LEARN
TO PLAY
COUNTRY
GUITAR

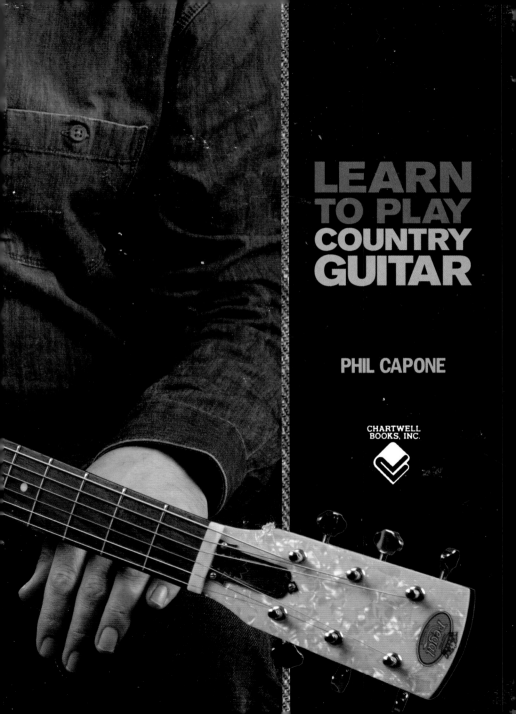

LEARN
TO PLAY
COUNTRY
GUITAR

PHIL CAPONE

CHARTWELL
BOOKS, INC.

A QUARTO BOOK

Published in 2012 by
Chartwell Books, Inc.
A division of Book Sales, Inc.
276 Fifth Avenue, Suite 206
New York, New York 10001
USA

Copyright © 2012 Quarto Inc.

ISBN: 978-0-7858-2901-0
QUAR.LPCG

Conceived, designed,
and produced by
Quarto Publishing plc
The Old Brewery, 6 Blundell Street
London N7 9BH

Project editor: Lily de Gatacre
Art editor: Joanna Bettles
Designer: Anna Plucinska
Copy editor: Caroline West
Photographer: Martin Norris
Assistant art editor: Kate Bramley
Indexer: Ann Barrett

Art director: Caroline Guest
Creative director: Moira Clinch
Publisher: Paul Carslake

Color separation in Hong Kong by
Modern Age Repro House Limited
Printed in China by Midas Printing
International Limited

10 9 8 7 6 5 4 3 2 1

CONTENTS

INTRODUCTION

The term "country music" covers a huge number of styles and sub-genres and can be played on acoustic guitar, electric guitar, pedal steel guitar, or resonator guitar. Then there's a long list of techniques that include strumming, fingerpicking, hybrid picking, string bending, slide, and more. That's a pretty exhausting set of skills to learn, not to mention one hell of a shopping list! Some might say that it's impossible to cover all of the fundamental country techniques in a single guitar book. However, the goal of this book is not to make you a virtuoso player, but to make you fluent in a wide range of techniques. Apart from specific electric-guitar-focused skills such as double-stop string bending, all of the lessons can be played on a good old-fashioned, flat-top, acoustic guitar. Even the lessons focusing on slide technique have avoided the more traditional "lap slide" approach so that you can play them on whatever instrument you have to hand. So, whether you want to write country songs, record your own country demos, play in a semi-pro country band, or you just love country guitar, then this book is definitely for you!

There are thirty lessons in this book plus an extensive chord and scale reference section. The lessons start with the basics, then build your technique gradually using clear, easy-to-understand, step-by-step photographs that make learning each new skill easy and fun. The inclusion of both conventional and TAB notation helps to make your progress effortless and frustration-free, even if you can't read music. The accompanying CD also lets you hear exactly how each piece should sound once completed.

Finally, the handy and compact form makes this book "guitar-case friendly," so you can take it with you wherever you go. The spiral binding means you can open it out flat, so it's a pleasure to use and guaranteed to make your practice sessions productive. So, grab your guitar and let's get started.

ABOUT THIS BOOK

This book is designed to help you learn to play country guitar the fun way. To get the most from the book, progress through the thirty lessons to develop your country-guitar techniques and pick up some important tips. Use the extensive chord and scale resources at the back of the book to enhance your skills and you'll become a confident, fluent player before you know it.

Lessons (pages 12–149)

Through these thirty lessons, the combination of short exercises, notation busters, and tunes to master, all clearly explained and demonstrated through photographs, will have you playing like a pro in no time.

Six lessons throughout the book will give you the chance to expand on the short exercises and work through a full 8- or 16-bar tune.

When you see this icon, listen to the track number listed on the CD at the back of the book to hear the exercise played for you.

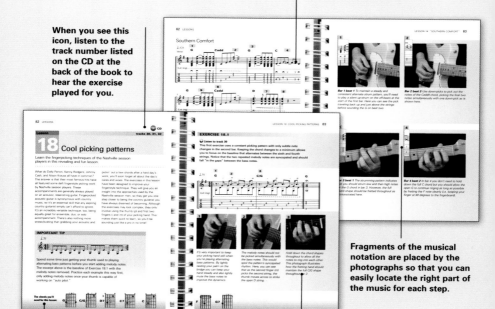

Fragments of the musical notation are placed by the photographs so that you can easily locate the right part of the music for each step.

The chords you will need for each lesson are shown at the bottom of the page in neat diagrams. See page 12 for a key to what the different colors mean.

Clear step-by-step photographs illustrate right- and left-hand techniques and highlight tricky spots to look out for within each short exercise.

Chord Library (pages 150–175)

A useful library of sixth, seventh, ninth, and diminished chords follows to help you expand your country chord vocabulary. See page 150 for a guide to the information that is included on the diagrams.

Chords are arranged by root chord which is spelled out in the top corners.

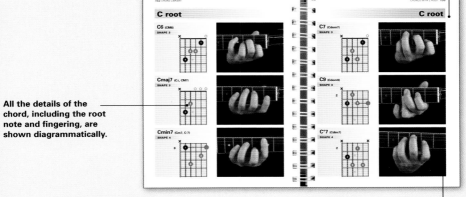

All the details of the chord, including the root note and fingering, are shown diagrammatically.

Each chord in the pentatonic scale library is "spelled out" from its root note with the intervals marked.

Photographs help explain the correct fingering and also allow you to check your chord shape looks right.

Scale Libraries (pages 176–251)

Two extensive scale libraries covering major and minor pentatonic scales, as well as open tuning are essential resources for the country guitarist. See pages 176 and 226 for notation guides to help you read the diagrams.

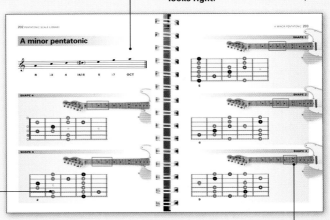

Easy-to-read, color-coded diagrams make it simple to locate root notes and get your fingering right.

A red "locator" box shows you exactly where on the guitar neck the scale is positioned.

THE FINGERBOARD

Finding notes on the fingerboard isn't easy; even accomplished players can be sketchy on this knowledge if they've learned primarily "by ear." This easy-to-use diagram will help you locate any note—and fast! Remember that after the twelfth fret the entire fingerboard repeats an octave higher (starting with the open string note name).

Fret 1
6 – F
5 – A#/Bb
4 – D#/Eb
3 – G#/Ab
2 – C
1 – F

Fret 2
6 – F#/Gb
5 – B
4 – E
3 – A
2 – C#
1 – F#/Gb

Fret 3
6 – G
5 – C
4 – F
3 – A#/Bb
2 – D
1 – G

Fret 4
6 – G#/Ab
5 – C#/Db
4 – F#/Gb
3 – B
2 – D#/Eb
1 – G#/Ab

FINGERBOARD REPETITION
The twelfth fret is the same as the open strings—from then on the notes repeat. For example, fret 13 is the same as fret 1.

Fret 5
6 – A
5 – D
4 – G
3 – C
2 – E
1 – A

Fret 7
6 – B
5 – E
4 – A
3 – D
2 – F♯
1 – B

Fret 9
6 – C♯/D♭
5 – F♯/G♭
4 – B
3 – E
2 – G♯/A♭
1 – C♯/D♭

Fret 11
6 – D♯/E♭
5 – G♯/A♭
4 – C♯/D♭
3 – F♯/G♭
2 – A♯/B♭
1 –D♯/E♭

Fret 6
6 – A♯/B♭
5 – D♯/E♭
4 – G♯/A♭
3 – C♯/D♭
2 – F
1 – A♯/B♭

Fret 8
6 – C
5 – F
4 – A♯/B♭
3 – D♯/E♭
2 – G
1 – C

Fret 10
6 – D
5 – G
4 – C
3 – F
2 – A
1 – D

Fret 12
6 – E
5 – A
4 – D
3 – G
2 – B
1 – E

OPEN STRINGS AND BARRE CHORDS
When a string is included in a chord without being fretted, it is called an "open string," indicated on the chord diagram by an "O." Strings not included at all are called out with an "X." Where two notes are joined by a bracket on the diagram, a barre chord should be played (see page 12).

LESSONS

Notation guide

Open position (first fret) chord box:

Chord box beginning on fifth fret:

5

✖ open string *not* played

O open string (root note) played

○ open string (chord note) played

● root note

● chord note

●━● barre or semi-barre

DIRECTIONAL SYMBOLS

You will see directional symbols just above the TAB stave.
A square symbol indicates down-picks and an arrow indicates
up-picks. The same symbols denote down-strums and up-strums.

⊓ down-pick or down-strum

V up-pick or up-strum

CHAPTER 1

This is the section of the book where you will learn all of the skills you'll need to become a proficient country guitarist. The lessons are progressive and designed to build your technique while you're playing and having fun! Every aspect of the genre is pretty much catered for and deals with specific acoustic, electric, and slide-guitar techniques. By the time you've completed all the lessons in this book, you'll know all of the essential tips and tricks that will enable you to play authentic country guitar.

To get the most out of this book, you should aim to review the previous lessons as often as you can, preferably at the start of every practice session. This will reinforce your knowledge and boost your confidence; you'll be amazing your friends with your newfound musical talents in no time!

RIGHT-HAND FINGER SYMBOLS

Abbreviations of the traditional Spanish names are used throughout for right-hand fingers; using numbers instead would create confusion with the fretting hand.

p (pulgar) = thumb
i (indice) = index
m (medio) = middle
a (anillo) = ring

Lesson

01 Choosing your guitar

If you haven't bought your guitar yet, or you're thinking of expanding your collection, this lesson will help you to make an informed choice.

Country is a very broad term that describes a huge catalog of music. Country music has many sub-genres and we will be exploring some, but not all of them, in this book. Because there are so many different styles of country music, and the guitar plays a pivotal role in all of them, different types of guitar

Legends and their guitars

The Pioneers of country guitar include such greats as Hank Williams who played a Gibson J45 Acoustic, a white Fender Stratocaster, or a Gibson Les Paul Custom. Chet Atkins often used a Gibson Chet Atkins CE with nylon strings, or, sometimes, a Country Gentleman, or a Super 4000. Merle Haggard used a Fender Telecaster, while Dwight Yoakam favored an Epiphone Casino since seeing the Beatles playing them. The spread of FM radio into rural areas in the 1990s brought an explosion in country music, with new artists such as Garth Brooks—who favors a Takamine GB-7C—and Billy Ray Cyrus—who plays a Gibson Deluxe Studio EC, a J-200, and a Dove. These artists took country music to a worldwide audience. After 2000, Black Shelton, who plays a Takamine solid top acoustic, had 17 singles on the country charts. In 2008 Taylor Swift, who has a customized Taylor Koa, was the biggest-selling musician in the US.

feature more heavily in some styles than in others. The four basic guitar types are: acoustic, resonator, electric, and pedal steel. The pedal steel guitar is a complicated and expensive instrument, and way beyond the scope of this book. However, you will learn some useful bending and slide techniques later on that can mimic the haunting sound of this instrument. You can play all of the pieces in this book on any acoustic, electric, or resonator guitar, but some of the techniques we will be exploring will sound more authentic on a

Gillian Welch playing her Gibson acoustic.

The legendary Garth Brooks is the number 1 selling solo artist in US history. Brooks is in the vanguard of the "new" country music, whose albums appeal to rock and country fans in about equal measure.

specific type of guitar. So, whether you already know which style of country guitar you want to play or not, this overview will help you to decide which guitar is best for you.

Acoustic Guitar

There are many different types of acoustic guitar, from the nylon-string type used in classical music to carved, archtop jazz guitars. As their name often suggests, each is suited to a specific genre. Traditionally, country guitarists have always played steel-string acoustic guitars, so this type of guitar was originally known as the western or country guitar. A steel-string guitar is more typically

used in supportive roles (i.e. strumming or fingerpicking), so it's ideal if you intend to accompany yourself or you just want to jam with a couple of friends. There are four standard body sizes: OO ("double oh"), OOO ("triple oh"), Dreadnought, and Jumbo, with OO being the smallest. It's only the body size that changes; the neck remains constant, so it's just a matter of picking the size that feels most comfortable to play. Obviously, the bigger the body, the bigger the sound, but the trade-off will be a less comfortable, bulky instrument (bigger body sizes also make the neck seem further away—not ideal for a beginner). The main drawback of the acoustic guitar is that in order to generate an authoritative sound, it is traditionally fitted with heavy-gauge strings and usually has quite a high action (this is the distance between the strings and the fingerboard). This is fine for strumming, fingerpicking, or slide work, but if you want to play lead lines or solos you'll find it's hard work. This is where an electric guitar comes into its own, especially when string bending. If you have no desire to play solos and just want to create mellow accompaniments, then the steel-string acoustic is for you.

Resonator/Dobro Guitar

The resonator guitar, also known as a *dobro* guitar, produces greater volume levels than a regular acoustic so it's ideal for playing solos and melodies, especially with a slide. Plucking a string causes a metal cone (or cones) to resonate and so produces a naturally amplified sound, hence the guitar's name. The resonator guitar has a very distinctive sound that features heavily in country music, particularly in

Famous resonator guitarist and producer Jerry Douglas (of the Alison Krauss band) playing a square-neck resonator.

bluegrass styles. There are two basic designs of resonator: square-necked guitars that are played lap-style with a slide; and round-necked guitars that can be played lap-style or conventionally, with or without a slide. Although many bluegrass players favor the square-neck type of guitar for slide work this, like the pedal steel guitar, is a very specialized way of playing and beyond the scope of this book. So, we'll be exploring the resonator examples in this book on a round-necked guitar played in the conventional way. The aim of this book is to give you a taste of as many different styles of country guitar as possible, without straying too far from conventional techniques or the need for specialist instruments. Buy a resonator guitar if you love the quirky, metallic sound that it produces. They are great for strumming, fingerpicking, or slide work but, like the steel-string acoustic, you will find the heavier strings a handicap when playing melodic techniques such as bends, hammer-ons, and pull-offs.

Electric Guitar

The electric guitar is without doubt the most versatile of the three types of guitar featured here. It can be used to provide accompaniment, to play melodies, or to play full-blown solos. You can play it quietly in the privacy of your own home; or you can take it to a jam session, turn your amp up loud, and stun the crowd with your hot country licks. The disadvantage of an electric guitar is that it hardly makes any sound at all when it's not plugged into an amplifier, so you'll need to figure one of these into your budget. However, if you only intend to use your guitar at home, you could get by with an inexpensive headphone amplifier that plugs directly into your guitar's output socket (they usually have an auxiliary input that allows you to jam with an external audio player too). There are also computer interfaces (again these can be small and inexpensive) that will allow you to use your computer as a virtual amplifier or recording studio (you will need to buy additional software to do this though).

There is a bewildering array of electric guitars on the market today, so which type is best for country music? Without question the instrument most widely used by country players is the ubiquitous Fender Telecaster. It has a range of tones that are perfectly suited to country music; you can even buy them with a "B-bender" fitted, a mechanical device that can bend the second string sharp when you push down on your guitar strap. This allows you to execute complex, double-stop bends that replicate the sound of a pedal steel guitar. The B-bender has consequently been a favorite of Nashville session players since the 1960s. Fender have always offered a good range of Telecasters in their catalog. It's been their second most popular model (next to the Stratocaster) since the 1950s, so you're bound to find one that suits your taste and budget. The Squire series has been Fender's budget series since the 1980s; these guitars are manufactured outside of the USA to keep costs down. American-built Fenders are more expensive, with the top-of-the-range "custom shop" models commanding serious money. Because of the Telecaster's very simple bolt-on neck design, you could even buy all of the components (body, neck, pickups, etc.) separately from licensed suppliers such as Allparts and build your own custom model.

Above right: Brad Paisley playing his famous Crook Blue Paisley custom Fender Telecaster.

Right: Merle Haggard playing his Fender Telecaster.

Reading the dots

Don't worry if you can't read music, reading TAB is easy!
This lesson shows you how...

Every example in this book has been annotated using a combination of conventional notation (what musos call "the dots") and TAB (short for "tablature"). The majority of guitar publications use this system, so you're probably already comfortable with it. If you're not, don't worry; this lesson will explain everything you need to know. While it's not necessary to be able to read conventional notation to get the most from this book, you'll find a little time spent now on understanding the basics will be well worth it. Conventional notation is extremely useful in two areas: 1) for describing rhythmic content and 2) for adding fretting-hand fingerings. None of this important information can be conveyed when using TAB alone.

EXAMPLE 1

The traditional five-line stave is not guitar specific; it can be used for any musical instrument that reads from the treble clef (some instruments read from different clefs that then change the range of notes on the stave). Each line and space has a corresponding letter name representing a specific pitch.

EXAMPLE 2

In this example, you can see how the six lines of the TAB stave represent the six strings of the guitar, starting with the lowest (E) at the bottom. To read TAB all you have to do is convert the number on the line to a fret on the corresponding string, easy!

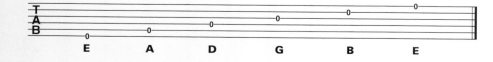

EXAMPLE 3

In this example, a stave of conventional notation has been added above the TAB stave. You can see how easy it is to find the notes from Example one when the conventional notation has a stave of TAB added below it.

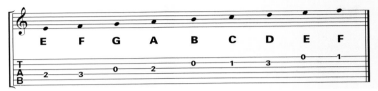

EXAMPLE 4

Here you can see how the notes written in conventional notation describe duration (i.e. rhythm) as well as pitch. With a little practice you'll soon be able to identify rhythms by sight.

| whole note = 4 beats | half note = 2 beats | quarter note = 1 beat | eighth note = ½ beat | 16th note = ¼ beat |

EXAMPLE 5

For each of the notes above there's an equivalent rest as you can see below. Don't forget: it's not what you play but what you leave out that counts.

| whole rest = 4 beats | half rest = 2 beats | quarter rest = 1 beat | eighth rest = ½ beat | 16th rest = ¼ beat |

EXAMPLE 6

In this final example, a simple three-note riff has been clearly notated using a combination of TAB and conventional notation. The first two notes are quarter notes and last one beat each; the last note is a half note and should ring for two beats. Notice that fretting-hand fingering detail has also been included beneath the notes in the top stave. By referring back to the stave in Example 1, you will also see that the pitches are D, E, and F respectively.

Lesson

03 How to hold your guitar

Time spent improving your posture, whether you're
sitting or standing, is time well spent.

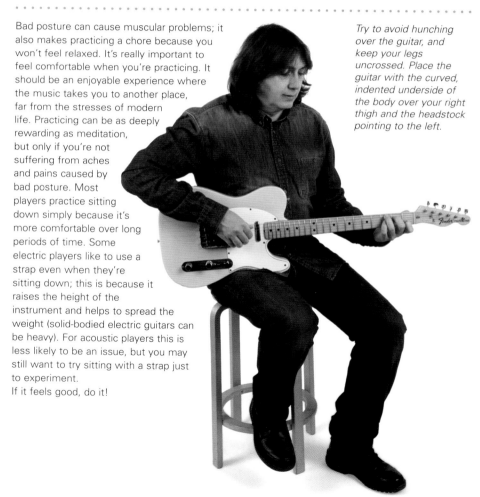

Bad posture can cause muscular problems; it
also makes practicing a chore because you
won't feel relaxed. It's really important to
feel comfortable when you're practicing. It
should be an enjoyable experience where
the music takes you to another place,
far from the stresses of modern
life. Practicing can be as deeply
rewarding as meditation,
but only if you're not
suffering from aches
and pains caused by
bad posture. Most
players practice sitting
down simply because it's
more comfortable over long
periods of time. Some
electric players like to use a
strap even when they're
sitting down; this is because it
raises the height of the
instrument and helps to spread the
weight (solid-bodied electric guitars can
be heavy). For acoustic players this is
less likely to be an issue, but you may
still want to try sitting with a strap just
to experiment.
If it feels good, do it!

*Try to avoid hunching
over the guitar, and
keep your legs
uncrossed. Place the
guitar with the curved,
indented underside of
the body over your right
thigh and the headstock
pointing to the left.*

Experiment with your strap and keep adjusting it until you're comfortable. There's no optimum position, as this varies from player to player. Avoid wearing the guitar too low—it may look cool but it's really bad news for your fretting hand.

IMPORTANT TIP

You may be tempted to skip this lesson but spending time on your posture is time well spent. An awkward playing position makes practicing hard work, meaning you'll spend less time with your instrument. So, learning how to hold your guitar correctly will, without question, make you a better player.

CD

Tune up!

An out-of-tune guitar will make you sound bad, so it's well worth taking time out to learn how to tune efficiently.

All too often guitar students overlook their instrument's tuning because they don't want to waste valuable practice time on "chores." Playing an out-of-tune guitar not only makes whatever you play sound terrible, it will also inhibit your aural skills (developing a good "ear" is essential to being a good musician), and it could even damage your guitar. Guitar strings are under a lot of stress, so even an expensive, top-quality instrument won't stay in tune for long. Get into the habit of checking your tuning *every* time you pick up your guitar.

Tuning by ear

This method is called "relative tuning" since it only verifies that the guitar is in tune with itself (as opposed to being in concert pitch). The TAB below shows you how you can check each pair of strings to make sure they're nicely in tune. Each pair of notes produces the same pitch as indicated above the TAB, so play the strings simultaneously for the best results. When the strings are nearly in tune, you will hear a beating or pulsating effect caused by the slight difference in pitch. As the pitches get closer, the beating slows and will disappear altogether when the strings are completely in tune.

Using a tuner

An electronic tuner will keep your guitar in concert pitch. This is not only important for playing with other musicians; it also avoids putting too much (or too little) stress on the guitar's neck, which can cause it to bend out of shape. Electric guitars (or acoustic guitars fitted with a pickup) can be plugged directly into a tuner. Most tuners also have a built-in mic for tuning acoustic instruments. Some tuners clamp onto the guitar's headstock and tune by picking up the strings' vibrations. The tuner will indicate whether the string is in tune, sharp, or flat, so all you have to do is adjust the appropriate machine head (tuning peg). If your guitar is a long way out of tune, an electric tuner may not be able to identify the pitch of the string correctly. If this happens, don't be afraid to ask your local music store (or a guitar-playing friend) for help.

On the CD – Track 1

🎧 To help you get in tune we've included some tuning notes on the accompanying CD—each string is played three times starting with the first (high E) string.

IMPORTANT TIP

Learning to tune quickly and efficiently will make you a better musician. You can spend less time tuning and more time playing, and the music you create will sound much sweeter! If you're using an electronic tuner, make sure that the guitar's volume is turned up full. When you're using the tuner's built-in mic, rest the tuner on your leg as close to the guitar's soundhole as possible.

Pick the string that you're tuning repeatedly, but not too quickly. Avoid hitting neighboring strings or the tuner won't be able to identify the pitch.

Turn the machine head slowly as you play the string—you'll probably only have to move it a fraction of a turn.

Lesson 05

The picking-hand position

Country guitarists use a variety of picking techniques, so this lesson will be core to your development, and one you'll probably want to refer back to quite frequently.

In this lesson we'll be learning how to develop an efficient picking-hand technique. Because it's natural to look at your fretting hand when you're practicing, it's almost inevitable that you're likely to overlook (quite literally!) your picking-hand technique. Unfortunately, many students attach too little importance to their picking-hand technique, realizing only too late that bad habits have been learned. There's nothing worse than having to unlearn part of your playing style and repair bad techniques in order to move forward; it can be very frustrating. So, as is the case with all of these early lessons, it's very important not to be tempted to just get "stuck in" and skip to the playing parts.

EXERCISE 5.1

Standard technique
The simplest and most commonly used technique for sounding the strings is to strike them with a pick (plectrum). This can seem rather unnatural to the novice and, because it's difficult to see what's actually going on when watching a guitar player live or on TV, it's easy to fall into bad habits early on. Pickstyle notation uses a square symbol (⊓) to indicate down-picks and an arrow (V) to indicate up-picks just above the TAB stave as illustrated below (see page 12). These symbols may also indicate down- and up-strums when playing chords.

Grasp the pick between your thumb and first finger. Notice how little of the pick remains visible and how it protrudes at a right angle to the thumb—the more of the pick you are holding, the easier it is to control.

EXERCISE 5.2

Fingerpicking

The general rule for fingerpicking is to use the thumb (*p*) to play bass notes (generally on strings four, five, and six), while the first three fingers (*i*, *m*, and *a*) pick out melody and chord notes on the upper strings (see page 13). Independence between the thumb and fingers is crucial so it's important to develop a good technique. Fingerstyle notation uses downward stems to indicate bass notes, while melody notes have upward stems. It is common practice to add picking-hand finger indications (*i*, *m*, and *a*) next to the relevant melody notes (see below).

When fingerpicking, the hand should be suspended above the strings with the thumb remaining parallel to the bass strings. Keeping the fingers in a claw-like shape allows them to pick the strings without the hand moving.

EXERCISE 5.3

Hybrid technique

This technique is widely used by country guitarists since it allows double stops (i.e. two notes played together) to be easily played. Hybrid picking is, as its name suggests, a mixture of pickstyle and fingerpicking; a lower string is picked conventionally (i.e. with the pick) while the second finger (*m*) simultaneously picks a higher string. Hybrid picking is notated in the same way as regular pickstyle but with picking-finger notation (*m* and/or *a*) added next to the relevant notes in the notation, as in the example below.

Here is a clear example of hybrid picking in action with the pick striking the third string while the second finger (m) simultaneously picks the first string.

Lesson

06 The fretting-hand position

An efficient fretting-hand technique will allow you to play with less effort—so you can concentrate on making sweet music!

Country guitar is a popular music genre but that doesn't mean it's any less demanding to play than more "serious" forms of music like jazz and classical. So, it's really important to concentrate on developing a good all-round technique in both hands. It may seem rather fussy to worry about your hand position when you're just getting started, but by establishing good habits now you'll be laying the foundations for a lifetime of frustration-free playing. Developing an efficient fretting-hand technique is very important; you'll be able to play with less effort if your picking hand is working at maximum efficiency, and you'll also

The thumb should be positioned in the center of the neck—this will provide maximum support for the fingers when you're pressing down on the strings. It also ensures that your palm stays off the neck.

Many country players occasionally use the thumb to play bass notes on the sixth string— this is fine, but make sure you always return to the default position described to the left to avoid straining your hand.

Always try to keep your left-hand thumb positioned in the center of the neck. Think of this as a default position that you should always return to—even if you occasionally use your thumb to fret notes on the sixth string. Remember that good technique is essential for making good music.

achieve better, and, ultimately, more professional-sounding results. If you can change chords without leaving big gaps, allow fretted notes to ring for their full value, and play accurate bends, slurs, and slides, you'll really start to sound like a true Nashville session player.

The tip of your finger should approach the fingerboard directly from above and ideally at a 90-degree angle (to avoid damping adjacent strings). It's also important to place your finger close to the fret to avoid weak, buzzy-sounding notes.

Aim to keep your fingers hovering above the strings when they're not fretting. This cuts down the movement required to fret a note and also means that you will be able to play with less effort.

CD

tracks 2, 3, 4

Easy strumming patterns

Three easy-to-learn strumming patterns to help you to build your accompaniment skills.

The "bread-and-butter" of country guitar playing is all about being a great rhythm player. Sure, nothing beats a cool solo, but if you can't lay down a solid rhythm part, then you won't be very popular at jam sessions! You can see from the chords listed at the bottom of this page that we're keeping the shapes nice and simple; playing good rhythm is all about keeping good time, not about playing fancy chord shapes. So, the focus for this lesson will be on your picking hand and the importance of keeping your arm moving steadily up and down like a metronome to achieve even and consistent strumming patterns. You should find this quite easy to achieve in the first two exercises, but when a little syncopation (the emphasis of weak beats) is introduced in the last exercise, you may find things get a little trickier. But take your time, practice with a metronome, play along with the backing track, and you'll soon be strumming like a pro! It's also a good idea to go to some gigs so you can check out how other guitar players do it; nothing beats watching other musicians playing in front of you for picking up tips and tricks. Good players will always keep their picking hand moving consistently, traveling the same distance every time.

Repeat bars

A thick line followed by a thin line and two dots is a repeat bar line. Always repeat whatever is between repeat bar lines (the repeated section can also consist of multiple bars as you'll see in this lesson).

IMPORTANT TIP

You'll notice that each exercise has a tempo marking above the first bar. This is the tempo of the recording on the CD. If you want to maximize the benefits from this lesson, then you should practice these examples at a variety of tempos. Remember that practicing with a metronome will improve your sense of rhythm and time, and ultimately *make you a better player*.

The chords you'll need for this lesson:

Am D G C D7

EXERCISE 7.1

🎧 **Listen to track 2**

Keep your strumming hand constantly moving down and up in a pendulum-like motion, hitting the strings only on the down beats. The up-pick does not make contact with the strings at all—this is called a *ghosted* strum.

Because the sixth string is not part of the chord, you can use your thumb to mute it as is shown here.

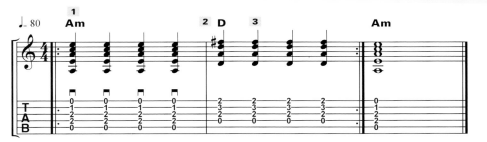

When changing shapes to the D chord, you'll need to move all three fingers quite quickly; do this at the end of the first bar rather than at the start of the second.

The fifth and sixth strings need to be omitted from your strum when you're playing the D chord, so try to "aim" your pick toward the higher strings.

EXERCISE 7.2

🎧 **Listen to track 3**
As in the previous exercise, this rhythm pattern requires you to keep your strumming arm moving constantly and evenly throughout. The first two strums are simple down-picks as before but on beats 3 and 4 you'll need to allow the up-picks to make contact with the strings as indicated by the picking symbols above the TAB.

The G chord should be played using the fingering shown here, i.e. with your second and third fingers on the lowest strings and your fourth finger on the first string. This will enable you to change quickly to the C chord in the second bar.

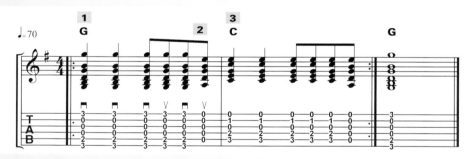

When playing eighth-note rhythms it's common practice to strum the open strings while your fingers are changing shapes. Because the notes fall on the off-beat at the end of the first bar they will not sound discordant.

When you're using the recommended G chord fingering it's easy to change quickly to the C—shift your second and third fingers onto the fourth and fifth strings and add your first finger to the second string.

EXERCISE 7.3

🎵 **Listen to track 4**

This last exercise has a more involved strumming pattern because it introduces syncopation on the third beat of each bar. Syncopation is what gives music "groove" because it emphasizes the weak beats (in this case the off-beat on the third beat). You should have found it quite easy to "ghost" up-strums in the previous examples, but ghosting down-strums feels less natural. Take your time and remember to keep that strumming arm moving constantly.

This exercise adds a ghosted down-strum on beat three—these are much harder to play, so don't worry if you find this difficult at first. Start slow and make sure you keep your strumming arm moving down and up throughout.

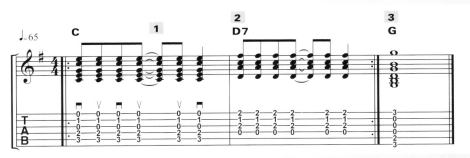

When you change to the D7 chord in the second bar, keep your first finger in position on the second string, first fret—you only need to move your second and third fingers.

In this instance, the more familiar G chord fingering provides a nice, quick change to the final chord.

CD

 Lesson 08 **CD tracks 5, 6, 7**

Easy picking patterns

Three easy-to-learn picking patterns that will make you sound like a pro!

A strummed rhythm pattern is great for providing basic accompaniments, but when you need a little more sophistication nothing beats a cool picking pattern. A picking pattern is basically an arpeggiated chord, i.e. where the notes are picked out individually instead of being sounded simultaneously. It's important to allow the picked notes to ring into each other (otherwise you'll be playing an arpeggio), so remember to hold down the full chord shape while you're picking out the notes. There are three ways to play a picking pattern (see Lesson 5): 1) using your pick; 2) using your fingers; and 3) using a combination of pick and fingers (known as hybrid picking). The contemporary country guitarist needs to be fluent in each of these techniques, so this lesson aims to get you started. Each exercise relates to a specific technique (Exercise 8.1 using your pick, Exercise 8.2 using your fingers, and Exercise 8.3 using pick and fingers). As a general rule, the pick and hybrid picking approaches are more suited to electric guitar styles and ensemble work, while the fingerstyle approach is essentially an acoustic technique that's ideal for self-accompaniment. However, even if you're an electric player who rarely plays acoustic (or vice versa), there are likely to be scenarios (e.g. when overdubbing guitar parts on your latest home demo) where you'll be glad to have all three techniques, quite literally, at your fingertips.

IMPORTANT TIP

One of the most important skills a musician needs to develop is a rock-solid sense of time. This is essential not only for jamming with other musicians, but also for confidence and control when playing "tricky," off-beat syncopated notes (like the bass notes in Exercise 8.3). Try saying the word "and" after the number of each beat (i.e. "one and, two and", etc.) when you're counting time as shown below. This will enable you to accurately place the notes that fall in the gaps:

1 + 2 + 3 + 4 +

The chords you'll need for this lesson:

 C

 F

 Am

 D

 G

EXERCISE 8.1

🎧 **Listen to track 5**

When you're picking across the strings, it's easier to use consecutive down- or up-picks as in this example. The trade-off is that it's harder to maintain an even and consistent rhythm, so, as always, make sure you practice with a metronome.

You'll need to "jump" over the fourth string with your pick after you've played the first note. Here, you can see the pick in position ready to play the open third string on the second beat of bar 1.

Switch to up-picks after you've played the high E on the first string. Here the pick is poised and ready to strike the second string as it descends through the C chord halfway through the third beat.

To play the melody note in the second bar, keep the chord shape intact while adding the D on the second string with your fourth finger as indicated in the notation.

EXERCISE 8.2

🎧 **Listen to track 6**

For this exercise you'll be ditching that pick and switching to fingerstyle. Don't forget that it's worth experimenting with thumb and/or finger picks if you have a problem growing (and keeping) your picking-hand nails long; these have been used by many famous country pickers.

Keep your picking hand in position above the strings throughout as shown above. Your (i), (m), and (a) fingers pick the same strings throughout and should remain in position above their respective strings (i.e. the third, second, and first strings).

In the second bar your thumb moves one string higher in order to play the opening bass note of the D chord. Your fingers (i, m, and a) pick the top three strings as they did in the first bar.

One advantage of playing fingerstyle is that you don't always need to fret the full chord shape. Here, you can see the G is achieved by simply fretting the sixth string on the third fret.

EXERCISE 8.3

🎧 **Listen to track 7**

Although this notation looks rather involved, don't be put off—it's not as difficult as it looks! Play all the notes on the fourth and fifth strings with your pick (using down-picks) and all the notes on the second string with your second picking-hand finger (*m*). Notice how the bass notes are syncopated; they always fall "in the gaps" between the melody notes.

As you pick the first bass note, your second finger (m) should already be in position above the second string ready to play the double stop that follows.

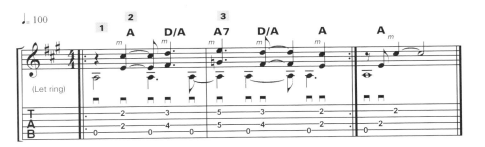

As you down-pick the fourth string on the second beat of the first bar, your second finger (m) simultaneously picks out the second string as illustrated here.

All of the double stops should be fretted with your second finger on the fourth string. Here you can see the A7 chord correctly played on the fifth fret at the start of bar 2 (the same fingering is also used for the A chord).

CD

"Truck Drivin' Man"

This original country tune will give your new accompanying skills a good workout while you play along to your own backing band.

One of the problems of learning new skills is that if you don't start using them immediately, they can quickly be forgotten. It's that "use it or lose it" scenario. That's why learning a musical instrument requires so much practice; it's all about programming your muscle memory system. However, that doesn't mean that a daily routine (and don't forget that "daily" is the ideal even if it's only 15 minutes)

The fermata sign

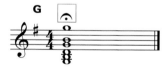

You've probably noticed that there's an unfamiliar symbol above the last chord in this tune. It's called a fermata sign and denotes that a note or chord should be allowed to ring past its written value. It's most commonly used in endings to provide a more satisfactory conclusion.

should consist of nothing more than repetitive scale practice. It's important to avoid making your practice sessions a chore—keep them fun and you'll keep playing and keep progressing. The best way to make your practice sessions more enjoyable and productive is to focus on a repertoire that incorporates the techniques you're currently working on. So, throughout this book, you'll find short tunes just like this one slotted in every few lessons, helping you to put your new skills into practice while you're making music. A desire to play music is, after all, the reason why we all pick up a guitar in the first place!

"Truck Drivin' Man"
Listen to track 8, play with track 9

This piece demonstrates how mixing and matching strumming with regular and hybrid picking techniques can create interesting accompaniments. Work through it methodically, isolating and repeating any problem areas that may arise. Don't forget that you should start well below the track tempo (try 70–80 bpm), notching up the speed gradually until you're able to play along with the backing track comfortably without making any mistakes. This progression would sound rather boring if it was

The chords you'll need for this lesson: **G**   **C/G**   **C**   **Am7**

simply strummed all the way through, but by adding the arpeggiated chords (bars 2 and 4) and hybrid-picked double stops (bars 5 and 6), variety and interest are created. The majority of country music is based around well-used chord sequences; it's the musicians that breathe life into them. So, remember that with a little creativity and imagination even the most tired and predictable of progressions can be transformed into something new, fresh, and exciting.

Be a better player

Tap your foot to keep time

To internalize the pulse of the music, always tap your foot while you're playing. It's important to use a metronome when you practice, making sure that your foot (and also what you're playing) is completely locked with it. If you find that you're losing time, then you'll need to reduce the tempo until you can play comfortably through each section. Remember that the tempo of the CD track is a target tempo; you're not expected to achieve this from the get-go.

Count and clap the rhythms

The most important element of music is rhythm. Without rhythm there would be no music, just a meaningless and jumbled collection of notes and chords. So, if you find yourself struggling with the rhythm (and we all do at some time or another), then take some time out before frustration kicks in. Put your guitar to one side and clap, tap, or sing the rhythm; you'll find that it's much easier to grasp when you're not trying to play the guitar at the same time. Remember that adding the "and" after each beat when you're counting will help you to place off-beat notes accurately as this excerpt (from bar 5) clearly illustrates:

Truck Drivin' Man

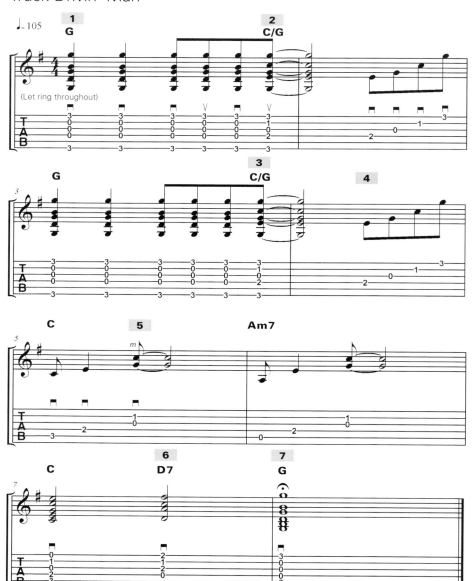

Bar 1 beat 1 *The G chord should be fretted with only your third and fourth fingers as shown here. Angle your third finger so that it just touches the fifth string and prevents it from sounding.*

Bar 1 beat 4 *To change to the C/G chord simply add your first and second fingers as shown here. Your third and fourth fingers should remain in position throughout the change of chord.*

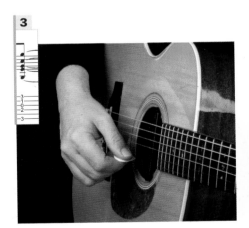

Bar 3 beat 4 *The C/G chord falls on the upbeat of beat four in bar 3, so it should be played with an up-strum as shown here.*

Bar 4 beat 3 *Traditionally, eighth notes are alternate picked but it makes more sense to use economy picking when picking ascending arpeggios. All four notes of the C/G arpeggio should be played using down-picks as indicated.*

Bar 5 beat 2 *Using your pick and (m) finger together you will be able to simultaneously pick the second and third strings to play the double stop on the second beat of bar 5. Remember that hybrid picking is an essential country technique!*

Bar 7 beat 2 *When you change to the D7 chord from the C chord, keep your first finger in place on the second string as shown here. You'll notice that the third finger has the furthest distance to travel and needs to "overtake" the second finger.*

Bar 8 beat 1 *For the final G chord you should revert to simple fingering using the first, second, and third fingers. This is by far the quickest way to change quickly from the D7.*

Lesson

10 The major pentatonic scale

The major pentatonic is the most widely used scale in country music—so, whatever you do don't skip this lesson!

Just as the minor pentatonic scale is an integral part of blues and rock music, so the major pentatonic is equally indispensable to the country guitarist. The blues is more harmonically ambiguous and so has a much "darker" sound than country music. In the blues, the so-called "blue notes" (i.e. the minor third, diminished fifth, and minor seventh) are superimposed over major chords by using the notes of the minor pentatonic and the minor blues scale. Country music tends to rely much more on the major pentatonic scale to create a "brighter", less complex tonality. The major pentatonic scale contains all of the chord tones of a major chord with the same root name, so it is the perfect choice for

creating riffs and licks. Most country guitarists add the minor third (A♯/B♭) to the scale to introduce a little dissonance and so create more interesting licks; the resulting six-note scale is referred to as the "major blues scale." The minor third is country music's "blue note" and tends to be used as a chromatic passing note (i.e. between the major second and major third intervals) or as a chromatic approach note (i.e. resolving quickly onto the scale note above or below), as opposed to being sustained over the chord as it would in the blues. Don't worry if this is all beginning to sound a bit too technical—you'll instantly recognize the sounds when we start playing some licks in later lessons.

Interval checker

R   2   3   5   6   Oct

The major pentatonic is a five-note scale. The notes of the major pentatonic are derived from the parent major scale. The pentatonic scale omits two notes of the major scale: the problematic perfect fourth and major seventh intervals. This creates a "fool-proof" scale that's perfect for creating melodies, riffs, and solos.

EXERCISE 10.1

🎵 **Listen to track 10**
This is the shape five, two-octave pentatonic scale in G major. When you're learning any new scale it's a good idea to begin and end on the root note so that you can hear it in the correct harmonic context. That's why this exercise starts and finishes on the second note of the shape; the low E is included only when descending.

Use the alternate picking indicated throughout. Here you can see the second note of bar 1 being correctly played with an up-pick.

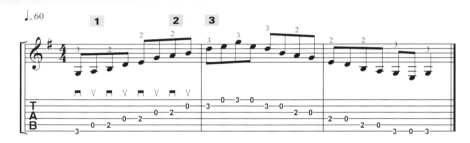

Keep your fingers in position above the strings throughout. Here you can see the second finger fretting the penultimate note of bar 1, with the remaining fingers in position above their respective frets.

Make sure your thumb is firmly placed on the back of the neck as illustrated in this photograph. Keeping it in this position allows all of your fingers to easily fret any note without having to move your hand.

EXERCISE 10.2

🎧 **Listen to track 11**

By adding the minor third (A♯ ascending, B♭ descending) passing note, the major pentatonic scale can be easily transformed into the major blues scale. Be sure to follow the fretting-hand fingering carefully as it is different when descending. For this exercise, the low E has been omitted to provide a logical resolution in bar 4.

Play the A♯ on the second beat of bar 1 with your first finger as shown here. Notice how the second finger is already in position above the second fret ready to play the B.

Continue for further steps ▶▶

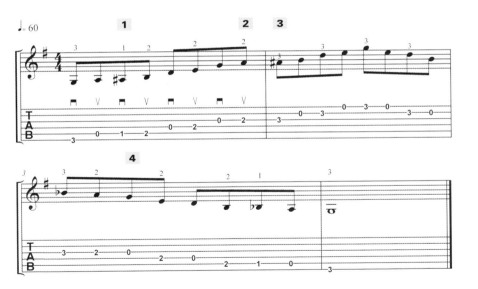

Remember to maintain alternate picking throughout with the up-picks falling on the off-beats. This photograph illustrates the third string correctly played with an up-pick at the end of the first bar.

This photograph illustrates the third finger fretting the A♯ at the beginning of bar 2. It will be released at the exact moment the following note (B) is picked to provide maximum note length and a smooth delivery.

Always make sure your fingers are in position, above the correct fret and string, ready to play the next note. Here the second finger hovers in readiness above the second fret (E) as the open G is played on beat two of bar 3.

IMPORTANT TIP

Five shapes are generated for every scale when using the CAGED system. In this lesson we'll be learning shape five (i.e. the "G shape") of the G major pentatonic scale. If this scale seems familiar, then that's because you probably already know the pattern as the E minor pentatonic scale. But, because the root notes are in different locations, a different set of intervals is generated, so the scale sounds completely different. You'll find all five shapes of the G major pentatonic scale in the Scale Library at the end of this book (see pages 176–225).

EXERCISE 10.3

🎧 **Listen to track 12**

By moving the previous pattern up to the twelfth fret, it can be transposed an octave higher. This is not only great for soloing, but it also converts the scale into a moveable shape so that it played in other keys. It's a good idea to practice the scale with and without the "blue" notes (A♯ ascending/B♭ descending) as you may not always want to include these in your licks.

In order to comfortably reach the notes on the twelfth fret, the first note should be played with your fourth finger as shown.

Continue for further steps ▶▶

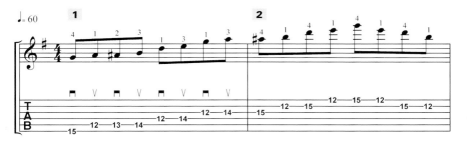

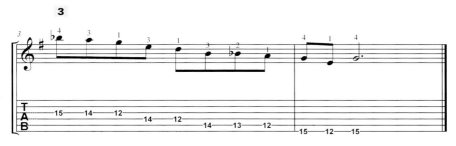

Alternate picking should be used throughout; so the first note of each bar should fall on a down-pick when played correctly. Here you can see the first note of the second bar correctly played with a down-pick.

As you fret the B♭ with your fourth finger on beat one of bar 3, your third and first fingers should also be in position above their respective frets as shown in this photograph.

James Burton was Elvis' guitar player for many years; he infused "The King's" music with cool country licks and riffs. Here you can see him playing his favorite guitar, the Fender Telecaster.

11   Adding bends, hammers, and slides

Expressive techniques such as string bending, hammering, and sliding are essential for playing cool country licks.

In this lesson you'll be learning how to play string bends and slurs; and I don't mean the way you might sound after sippin' a little too much good 'ole Tennessee whiskey! A string bend is fairly self-explanatory; it involves bending the string with your fingers to raise its pitch. A slur is a general musical term, used to describe legato phrasing on wind and stringed instruments. For guitar players this is achieved by picking only the first note of a sequence; the notes that follow are sounded with the fretting hand only, using hammer-ons, pull-offs, and slides. These are the techniques that the country guitarist uses to imitate the expressive

qualities of the human voice, to make their guitar talk, weep, and sing. Expressive techniques are therefore key to becoming an authentic country guitarist, so make sure you review this lesson frequently as you work through the book. These techniques will be featured heavily in later lessons. The following three exercises each deal with a specific technique, with clear instructions on how each one should be executed. It will take some time and practice before these techniques start sounding as they should, so be patient and you will be rewarded with the skills that will take your playing to a whole new level.

Notation buster

A straight line drawn between two different pitches indicates a slide. Like all of the examples here, these may also occur between several consecutive notes.

The slur symbol looks exactly like a tie, but it's only used between different pitches. It denotes a hammer-on (ascending) or pull-off (descending).

An "up" arrow followed by a specified interval indicates a bend-up. A "down" arrow indicates a pre-bend or bend release from the first pitch to the second.

EXERCISE 11.1

🎧 **Listen to track 13**

The slide is the easiest and most natural of expressive techniques to learn because it's what everyone does when they pick up a guitar for the first time: play along one string. The slide is not just a very useful expressive tool; it's also ideal for making slick position shifts up or down the neck. Make sure you allow each eighth note to ring for its full value before sliding your finger along the string.

IMPORTANT TIP

When you play a slide, only the first note should be picked, so make sure you keep your fretting finger firmly pressed down throughout the slide. If you release it (even slightly), you will mute the string and the second pitch won't be heard.

Use your first finger to fret all of the notes in this exercise. This photograph shows the first finger fretting the C on the first beat of bar 1.

You'll generate clearer notes by using down-picks when you play slides. Here you can see the second string is played with a down-pick at the start of the second bar.

It's important to keep your finger pressed down hard as you slide it along the string. This photograph captures the first finger "mid-slide" on the second fret as it moves down to the C at the end of the second bar.

EXERCISE 11.2

🎧 **Listen to track 14**

Unlike the other two techniques here, hammer-ons and pull-offs can be used with open strings as well as fretted notes. This makes them perfect for playing banjo-style rolls. In the first bar of this exercise, you'll be hammering-on and pulling-off using open strings. The second bar applies the technique to fretted notes, so remember that you need to fret both notes simultaneously.

IMPORTANT TIP

When you're playing a hammer-on or pull-off, remember that you won't be picking the second note. The pitch is generated solely by the motion of your fretting-hand finger. So, hammer-on the finger cleanly behind the fret, and pull-off with a quick, sideways, "flicking" motion.

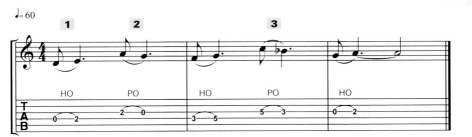

To play a hammer-on correctly, you need your fretting-hand finger to be ready, hovering above the string as shown here. Pick the first note and "hammer" your finger hard onto the string to generate the second pitch. Don't pick the second note.

Here you can see the second finger as it releases to the open G on beat three of the first bar. Notice how it has come to rest above the second string; that's because you need to release your finger with a sideways, "flicking" motion to generate the second note.

When applying the technique to fretted notes, the same "hammering" or "flicking" motion is used, but both notes must be fretted simultaneously. Here you can see the final pull-off on beat three of bar 2 with both the first and third fingers in position before the first note is picked.

EXERCISE 11.3

🎧 **Listen to track 15**

String bending is the hardest of the expressive techniques. Not only does it involve physically bending the string to change its pitch, but you'll also need to rely on your ear to tell you when you've hit the correct pitch or the note will sound terrible. As you can imagine this takes time and a lot of practice, but stick with it because string bending is the only way you'll achieve those haunting, pedal-steel-style country sounds.

IMPORTANT TIP

Bends are easier when played with three fingers; use your third finger to fret the note and add your first and second fingers behind it to provide extra strength. When learning to play bends, always check the pitch you are bending to by playing it first (e.g. to play a full two-fret bend from D to E, play the E first as a fretted note).

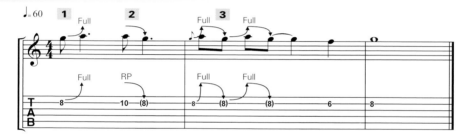

By placing three fingers on the string you'll find it's much easier to bend. Here you can see the third finger bending the second string up to an A on the first beat of bar 1, with the first and second fingers adding extra strength.

On the third beat of the first bar, the bend is held and re-picked (which is indicated by the "RP" above the TAB) before being released to its original pitch.

In the second bar a bend, release, and re-bend are all played without re-picking. This photograph shows the fingers have released the bend to the G before re-bending again to the A on beat two of the second bar.

Lesson

12 Easy pentatonic licks

Now you've got those major pentatonic shapes down, let's
put them to good use and start learning some licks!

Learning scales is a tedious but essential part
of musicianship but it's not until you start
needing them to play licks and solos that you'll
realize just how important they are. The major
pentatonic only consists of five notes, but an
endless number of cool country licks have
been created with it over the decades. Scales
on their own, of course, are not licks. To create
licks we need to add what is probably the
most important ingredient of music: rhythm.
You'll hear a lot of players talking about
"phrasing"; the pros know exactly how
important phrasing is. Just like a good
conversation, country lead guitar is all about

playing ideas that grab the listeners' attention.
It's about being in control of the groove,
knowing exactly which beat you're playing on,
and manipulating the "weak" beats to create
syncopations. Just think how boring music
would sound if notes could only be played on
the beat. By now you should be practicing
everything with a metronome ticking away in
the background. Very few people have perfect
"time." It's something all great musicians have
worked hard on and usually continue to do so
throughout their career. So if you're yet to start
practicing with one, turn over that new leaf
today—you won't regret it!

The 8va symbol

In Exercise 12.3 you'll notice there's an 8va symbol followed by a dotted
bracket over the whole lick. This means that it should be not be played as
written, but an octave higher. The TAB remains unaffected by this; it's purely
to make reading "the dots" easier. The bars above would sound identical, but
because of the absence of ledger lines in the first, it is much easier to read.

EXERCISE 12.1

🎧 **Listen to track 16**
This lick uses notes from the open shape five, G major pentatonic scale (see Exercise 10.1) to create a typical country phrase. Slurs (i.e. hammer-ons and pull-offs) are used throughout to make the phrase easier to play at brighter tempos. By repeating a three-note pattern as in this example (the first note of each group is marked by an accent), the phrase plays "across" the beat to create an exciting, syncopated lick.

IMPORTANT TIP

You'll notice two tempo markings are given for each of these three exercises. That's because each exercise is played twice: first at the slower tempo and second at the faster tempo. This doesn't mean you have to be able to play the faster tempo now. It's to let you hear how cool the lick sounds when played up-tempo. Be patient, practice these licks regularly, and in no time you'll be playing them at full speed.

Remember that when you play a hammer-on, you only pick the first note. The second pitch is generated by the force with which your finger hits the fingerboard. Here the second finger is poised and ready to hammer-on to the second note.

It's important to maintain the order of alternate picking (as indicated in the notation) when playing slurs. This photograph illustrates the third string (G) correctly played with an up-pick on beat three of bar 1.

When you play the B on the fifth string in bar 2, fret the note by laying your finger flat so that it gently touches the higher strings as shown here. This will damp the open third string and prevent it from ringing into the other notes.

EXERCISE 12.2

🎧 **Listen to track 17**

Once you've created a three-note pattern, the notes can be changed to provide a variation on the original idea. By removing the accents, the lick becomes less obvious; the phrase still generates syncopation but in a more subtle way. As in the previous exercise, the slurs produce a slicker delivery and make the lick much easier to play at "up" tempos.

IMPORTANT TIP

When your pick needs to travel across an un-played string to reach its destination (as in the second bar of Exercise 12.2), make sure you keep it nice and close to the strings as you move it. The more minimal your picking hand movements are, the more accurate your playing will be.

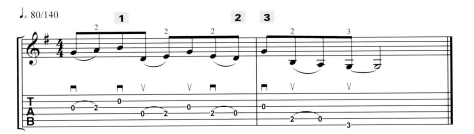

As you pick the second string on beat two of bar 1, your second finger should lift off the second fret to mute the previous note. Don't lift it high above the strings; aim to keep it just off the string as is being shown here.

Remember that when you're playing a pull-off, you need to flick your finger sideways when lifting it off the string. Here the second finger rests against the third string after playing the pull-off on beat four of bar 1.

There's a tricky string jump on the first beat of the second bar, so your pick needs to jump over the fourth string. This photograph captures the pick midway and directly above the fourth string as it moves toward the fifth.

EXERCISE 12.3

🎧 **Listen to track 18**

This final example is based on the transposed G major pentatonic that you learned in Exercise 10.3 (but with "blue notes" omitted). We'll also be using double-stop bends here for the first time. A double-stop bend involves holding the string-bend while you pick a second note. The two notes should ring simultaneously in order to emulate the sound of a pedal steel guitar.

IMPORTANT TIP

Double-stop bends should be played with your third finger fretting the bend and your fourth finger simultaneously fretting the higher string. The bend should be played with three fingers; use your third finger to fret the lower note, adding your first and second fingers behind for strength.

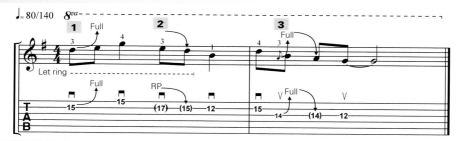

It's essential to use all four fingers when executing double-stop bends as shown in this photograph. This provides extra strength, enabling you to hold the note at its bent pitch while fretting the higher note with your fourth finger.

Before releasing the double-stop bend it should be re-picked (indicated by the "RP" above the TAB). The fourth finger should remain in position as shown, allowing both notes to continue ringing simultaneously.

The picking hand should adhere to alternate picking throughout. Here you can clearly see the second note of bar 2 being correctly played with an up-pick.

CD

Lesson

13 Easy blues scale licks

Learn how to use the major blues scale to create
exciting and authentic country licks and solos.

Learning licks is an essential part of learning to play country guitar. They're absolutely vital if you're yearning to be in the spotlight, playing a cool solo and momentarily stealing the attention from the singer. Even if you have no such aspirations, the guitar is capable of so much more than just providing a strummed accompaniment; it would be a great shame not to learn how to manipulate its more expressive qualities. The origins of country music can be traced back directly to the early American immigrants who settled in the Kentucky Mountains. The music they played was bluegrass, and many critics argue that this is the "real deal." Once country music became

popular, the record companies took over and it lost its authenticity and honesty. The early bluegrass musicians had a very tough existence; it would have been an unimaginably hard life by today's standards, so they only had the most basic of instruments at their disposal. Guitars would have been a luxury, so many of the country licks we hear today started out on the banjo. The major blues scale will get you closer to the original bluegrass sound than any other scale. In these examples, you'll not only learn how to create bluegrass-flavored licks, but also how add pedal-steel-style, double-stop bends into the mix in order to create super-cool country licks.

Interval checker

* = **Minor third ("blue" note)**

| R | 2 | ♭3 | 3 | 5 | 6 | Oct |

The major blues scale is an unusual six-note scale. Not just because it has six notes, but also because it contains both the major and minor third intervals. When you're using this scale it's important to remember that the minor third should not be directly sounded against the tonic chord. It's much more effective when used as a passing note (i.e. between the major second and major third) or as a chromatic approach note (i.e. immediately followed by the major second and major third).

EXERCISE 13.1

Listen to track 19
This lick is based on the open, shape-five G major blues scale shape that you learned in Lesson 10. It's a simple question-and-answer-type phrase with the first bar climbing through the scale and the second bar descending to its natural conclusion back home on the root. Notice that there's only one slur at the end of the second bar, and none in the first bar, so this will require accurate picking at full tempo.

IMPORTANT TIP

Just as in the previous lesson, there are two tempo markings for each exercise. The faster tempo marking has increased to 160 bpm. This gives you a starting tempo that is at half speed. The tempo should only be increased gradually over several practice sessions. This may take some time, but be patient and you will be rewarded with slick licks!

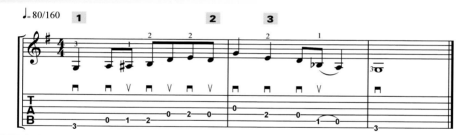

As you fret the first note with your third finger, your first finger should also be in position above the first fret, ready for the A♯ on the second beat.

Always try to minimize the distance that your pick travels when using alternate picking. Here you can see the pick momentarily at rest after playing the E at the end of the first bar; it's already in position and ready to re-pick the open string.

As you fret the E on beat two of the second bar, angle it slightly, just enough to make contact with the third string. By lightly touching it you will mute it and so prevent it from ringing through the second bar.

EXERCISE 13.2

🎧 **Listen to track 20**

When you're playing a lot of slurs, as in this example, it doesn't always make sense to use alternate picking. That's when using *economy picking* can offer greater picking efficiency, providing increased speed with less effort. Only the E on beat four of bar 1 and the final G deviate from the "pick down on the beat" philosophy of alternate picking, but once you've made these adjustments you'll find the lick can be played fast with minimal effort.

IMPORTANT TIP

Sometimes slurs are applied to consecutive notes as in this exercise. In this instance, you need to fret both notes before you play the first pull-off. Pick the string only once, flicking your second finger sideways as you release it to sound the second note, and then release your first finger sideways to sound the open string. Make sure you allow all the notes to ring for their full value.

This lick is played in second position (i.e. with the first finger starting on the second fret) so make sure that you fret the first note using your first finger as is shown here. Notice how the second finger is also in position above the third fret.

A double pull-off is used from the A♯ to G starting on the second beat of bar 1. Before you pick the first note, your first and second fingers should be in position on the string as is illustrated here.

The economy picking indicated (beat four, bar 1 and the final note of bar 2) disrupts the expected alternate picking patterns to facilitate a quicker, more relaxed delivery. Here you can see the final note (G) correctly played with a down-pick despite the fact that it falls on the off-beat.

EXERCISE 13.3

🎧 **Listen to track 21**
This final example is based on the G major blues scale on
the twelfth fret (Exercise 10.3). It incorporates double-stop
bends in the first bar to provide a nice contrast with the
distinctively bluegrass flavor of the second bar. Remember
that the notes should be allowed to ring until the bend
release is complete on beat three (indicated by the *let ring*
instruction above the TAB).

*When you're playing double-stop bends, fret
both strings simultaneously, even when the
higher string is not sounded immediately. Here
you can see the fourth finger already fretting
the high D as the third finger frets the A on
beat one.*

*As you release the double-stop bend, the
fourth finger must remain on the second string
as shown, allowing both notes to continue
ringing simultaneously.*

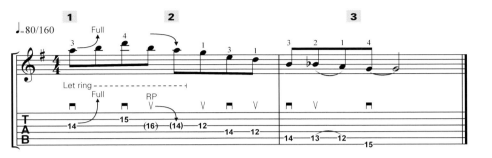

The picking hand sticks to alternate picking throughout apart from the final note. This can be played with a down-pick as indicated to provide a little extra "weight" to the lick's conclusion.

IMPORTANT TIP

If you're experiencing problems with string bending, then your strings may be too heavy. Try swapping the top three strings for lighter gauges (you don't have to change the whole lot). Some players even make up their own custom sets to make bends easier on the higher strings. Don't forget that string bending is much easier on an electric guitar, which doesn't need heavy strings to produce a big sound.

CD

tracks 22, 23

Lesson 14

"Southern Comfort"

This tune is great fun to play—it will also give the techniques you've learned so far in this book a thorough workout!

The contemporary country guitarist must not only be a "Jack of all trades" but a master of them too. Most importantly, the country guitarist has to be a great accompanist (this is true in every style of music) because country music is all about songs. It's that uncanny ability that all great session players have to play just enough and not too much, skillfully providing exactly the right amount of interest without ever becoming obtrusive. Of course, there's no denying that all guitarists love the chance to play a solo, but it's extremely important to be able to play solid rhythm work. That's what's gonna get you the gig and that's what's gonna put the beans on the table. Otherwise you'll find that, just like in the words of that classic Elvis song, "nobody wanted to hire a guitar man!" (By the way, it's the late, great Jerry Reed whose pickin' that cool guitar riff—he also wrote that tune.)

"Southern Comfort"
Listen to track 22, play with track 23
As your playing grows you need to be challenged by a more complex repertoire; in the early stages it's too daunting a prospect to be faced with long pieces of music; it could even make some fall at the first hurdle. But by now you are ready for something more substantial; that's why this tune is much longer (16 bars in total) than the first song you learned back in Lesson 9, "Truck Drivin' Man." In order to learn more efficiently, it's a good idea to break songs down into smaller sections, learning each one separately; it's that simple "bite off small chunks and they'll be easier to digest" kind of philosophy. You'll notice that the song naturally divides into two parts: verse and chorus. This breaks the piece into two eight bar sections which is better, but still too much to tackle in one practice session. If you study the verse section you'll notice that the first two bars are identical to bars 5 and 6. Always look for repeated ideas—it's a given in all popular music forms. So it makes sense to start with just the first two bars. When you've nailed this, move on to the next two bars and so on. If you work through the song methodically in this way, you will actually learn it more thoroughly and more quickly than by attempting to play through all of it in your first practice session.

The chords you'll need for this lesson:

G   Cadd9   C   D

Crescendo markings

In bar 7 you'll notice an unfamiliar symbol under the strummed D chord. This is a *crescendo* marking and indicates that you should increase the volume of the chord as you play. This is achieved by controlling the dynamics of your picking hand, starting softly and gradually increasing the force of your strumming hand. When the symbol is reversed you do the opposite, starting loud and then finishing softly. This technique is called *diminuendo*.

Staccato markings

When a dot is placed above or below a note, the note should be played shorter than its written value. When this is applied to a chord (as in bar 8 of this piece), the entire chord must be muted as soon as you've played it. When playing a moveable shape (i.e. with no open strings), you can do this by simply releasing the pressure of your fretting hand. This is less effective when dealing with chords that contain open strings; these are best muted by briefly touching the strings with your picking hand.

Southern Comfort

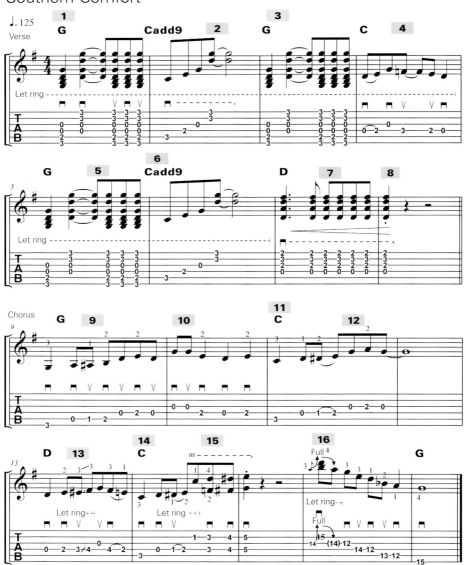

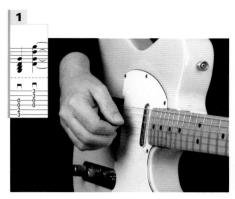

Bar 1 beat 1 *To maintain a steady and consistent alternate strum pattern, you'll need to play a silent up-strum on the off-beats at the start of the first bar. Here you can see the pick traveling back up and just above the strings before sounding the G on beat two.*

Bar 2 beat 3 *Use down-picks to pick out the notes of the Cadd9 chord, picking the final two notes simultaneously with one down-pick as is shown here.*

Bar 3 beat 1 *The strumming pattern indicates that you should strum low and then high notes for the G chord in bar 3. However, the full chord shape should be fretted throughout as demonstrated here.*

Bar 4 beat 2 *In bar 4 you don't need to hold down the full C chord but you should allow the open G to continue ringing as long as possible by fretting the F note cleanly (i.e. keeping your finger at 90 degrees to the fingerboard).*

Bar 5 beat 3 *Because the chord is not strummed on the third beat you'll need to play a "ghosted" down-strum to maintain the correct picking-hand rhythm. Play the strum with the pick just above the strings as shown in this photograph.*

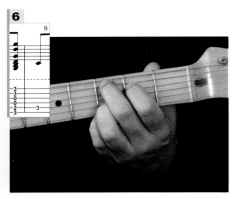

Bar 6 beat 1 *When you change from the G chord to Cadd9, only your first and second fingers should move. Keep your third and fourth fingers in position throughout, allowing the notes to continue ringing.*

Bar 7 beat 3 *The crescendo (see page 61) on the D chord in bar 7 should be played with down-strums throughout. This makes the dynamics easier to control and so produces a tighter sound.*

Bar 8 beat 1 *To dampen the D chord and play it staccato as indicated (see page 61), touch the strings with the side of your palm immediately after strumming the chord.*

Bar 9 beat 2 *To lift the chorus section, the guitar switches to single-note riffs. There are no slurs used in the first riff, so each note should be picked using alternate picking. This shot captures the A# on the second beat of bar 9 being correctly played with an up-pick.*

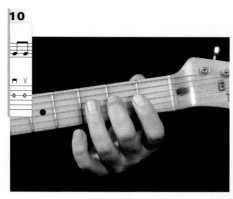

Bar 10 beat 1 *As you pick out the two open G notes at the start of bar 10, your second finger should be in position above the second fret, ready to play the E that quickly follows them.*

Bar 11 beat 1 *The riff under the C chord should be played in first position, starting with your third finger on the third fret of the fifth string as shown here.*

Bar 11 beat 3 *The alternate eighth-note picking should continue throughout bar 11. This shot shows the third string (G) being correctly played with an up-pick on the third beat.*

Bar 13 beat 2 The D riff in bar 13 starts in first position but uses the third finger to play both the E♯ and F♯, so you end up in second position. This photograph captures the third finger fretting the E♯ just before sliding up to the fourth fret to sound the F♯.

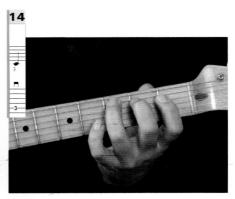

Bar 14 beat 1 Move back down to first position in bar 14, fretting the C on the fifth string with your third finger as shown here.

Bar 14 beat 4 The double stops at the end of bar 14 are played with hybrid picking. Pick the fourth string with a down-pick and simultaneously pick the second string by using your second fretting hand finger (m).

Bar 15 beat 1 The concluding lick starts with a double-stop bend that should be simultaneously fretted with your third and fourth fingers as shown here. The notes can be played with one down-pick (as indicated on the TAB) or by using hybrid picking.

Be a better player

Observing the "let ring" instruction

Unless you're following the direction of a staccato marking (see page 61), your playing will always sound more professional if you let every note ring for its full value. Sometimes you'll need to let the notes ring into each other, past their written value. This is usually indicated by a let ring instruction above the TAB. To do this, when you're strumming or picking out notes from a chord shape, hold the full chord shape until you've picked the last note to allow all the notes to keep ringing. Even un-played notes can resonate sympathetically, creating a fuller, richer chord. When you're playing single

notes (you'll see a shorter let ring bracket under the relevant section) this often involves letting the notes ring on adjacent strings as in bar 13 of "Southern Comfort" where the fretted F♯ on the fourth string rings into the open G on the string above. It's important that your fretting finger doesn't inadvertently damp the higher string in this instance, so keep your finger at 90 degrees from the fingerboard. You'll find that this is a recurring technique used by country guitarists (because it mimics the sound of a banjo) and so it's well worth getting it right.

CD

Lesson

15 Adding basslines

By picking out a bassline under a strummed chord you can add an extra dimension to your accompaniments.

By now you will be aware just how important it is to hone your accompaniment skills in order to become a good country player. There's one sure-fire way to lift your strumming patterns to make them sound slicker and more professional: just add some bass notes. This technique sounds cool either in a full rhythm section (as long as you're playing the same notes as the bass player!) or as a single guitar accompaniment. The basic principle of country bass playing is to play only on the first and third beats (or beats one and two in "cut time"—see below) of every bar. The first note is usually the root of the chord, and the second note is the fifth. So, basically, if you were to apply a root and fifth bassline to a

C chord, you'd hit the root note (C) on beat one and the fifth (G) on beat two, adding chord strums on the backbeat between the bass notes. The fifth is an important interval, so it's already included in most chord shapes; you just have to know where to find it. To work out which note is the fifth, simply count up four letter names from the root of the chord. So for a C chord, that's going to be a G. The G is the open third string in a C chord shape but you could also fret a low G on the sixth string, as we'll be doing later in the lesson. Eventually you'll instinctively know where to find the fifth of every chord; you won't even think about it, you'll just play it.

Cut time

Because country music is frequently played at fast tempos, it is often written and counted in *cut time*. Cut time is indicated by a 2/2 time signature. It contains exactly the same number of notes as a bar of 4/4, but the pulse is measured in half notes (as indicated by the bottom number of the signature) and not quarter notes as in 4/4. This means you only have to count two beats in every bar. It also means that you'll need to count eighth notes differently, as you can see below.

Count: 1   +   2   +   1   e   +   er   2   +

The chords you'll need for this lesson:

G   D   C

EXERCISE 15.1

🎵 **Listen to track 24**

With a little deft pick work, it's easy to pick out a country bassline from an open G chord. Since the chord is only strummed on the backbeat, this provides a self-contained country-style comp, perfect for self-accompaniment and duo work.

The full G chord shape must be held down throughout to allow all the chord notes to ring clearly.

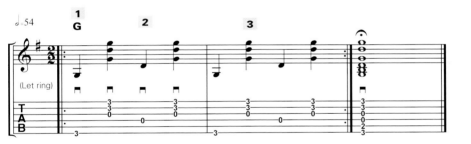

Because basslines sound better when the notes don't ring into each other, this comp will sound "tighter" if you lightly palm-mute the bass strings throughout as shown here.

Use down-strokes for all of the chord strums. This photograph illustrates the pick poised and ready to strike the G chord on beat two of the second bar.

EXERCISE 15.2

🎧 **Listen to track 25**
In this exercise we'll build on the previous idea by adding a chord change in the second bar. This will give you quite a lot to think about, so start your practice at a slower tempo, only notching up the speed gradually over several practice sessions.

Remember that quarter-note strum patterns should still be played with a down-strum in cut time. Here you can clearly see the pick ready to play the upper notes of the first G chord in bar 1.

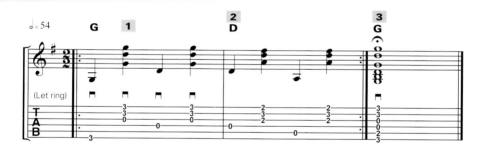

To avoid "choking" the G chord at the end of the first bar, you can postpone the change to the D chord shape because only the bass note is sounded on the first beat. This photograph shows the fingers forming the D shape as the open D string is picked.

Because the concluding G chord falls at the beginning of the first beat, you'll need to change quickly from the previous chord. Keeping your third finger in position as you move the other fingers will speed up the change, as shown here.

EXERCISE 15.3

🎧 **Listen to track 26**

It's not necessary to always add chord strums to your basslines. Sometimes you'll want to play a bass riff on its own, as in the second bar of this exercise. This would sound too busy if over-played in a song, so reserve ideas like this until the end of a verse or chorus section.

Although you're only picking out the low C note on the first beat of bar 1, you should fret the full chord shape to avoid any delay when playing the rest of the chord on the backbeat.

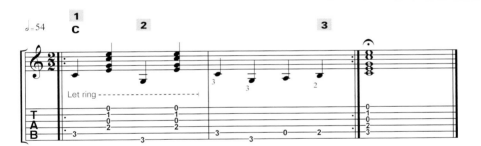

Instead of using the G contained within the chord shape, the fifth is played below the chord to add extra weight to the bassline. This involves moving your third finger onto the sixth string on the second beat as shown here.

The B note at the end of the second bar should be fretted with your second finger to allow a quick change back to the C chord. Notice how the third finger is hovering in anticipation of this change above the third fret.

CD

Lesson

16 Harmonizing melodies

tracks 27, 28, 29

Learn how to play tunes and chords simultaneously,
and max up your busking potential.

Having gotten this far in the book (and well done by the way!), you will have already acquired some very useful skills to help your playing sound more authentic. These have included a variety of picking approaches to provide more interesting accompaniments; cool string-bending tricks that emulate the pedal steel guitar; and sophisticated legato techniques to make your licks and solos come to life. But we've yet to tackle one of the guitar's most rewarding aspects: solo performance. This sounds scary but it really isn't—we're not talking concert-hall recitals here, just the skills that will enable you to pick out a melody while simultaneously adding a

few supporting chords. You can take this approach as far as you want, of course, but you'll find that it's very satisfying just picking out a simple tune while adding a few chords here and there. Your practice sessions will be all the more enjoyable because you'll be playing self-contained pieces of music. You'll also impress your friends because it's the tune that most people recognize; they won't care how clever your picking patterns are if there's no melody. And, just like the lesson heading says, you'll become a self-contained musician, so there's no excuse not to get out there and get playing.

The pause symbol

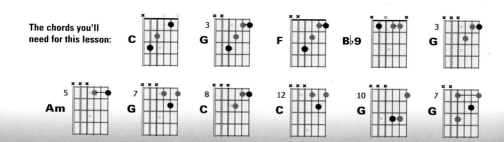

Two parallel dashes above the stave are an instruction to pause before playing the next note or chord. This shouldn't be held for too long; a fermata sign (see page 36) would be used to indicate a longer pause (as at the end of bar 2 in Exercise 16.3).

**The chords you'll
need for this lesson:** C   G (3)   F   Bb9   G (3)

Am (5)   G (7)   C (8)   C (12)   G (10)   G (7)

How to play melodies an octave higher

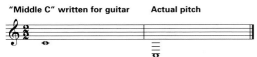

"Middle C" written for guitar   Actual pitch

Most folk don't realize that the guitar is a transposing instrument; it's actually written an octave higher than it sounds. This is to make the range of the guitar "fit" on one stave and make it easier to read. If you're reading music written by guitarists for guitarists, this will have already have been taken care off, but if you're reading tunes out of a songbook the melodies will be too low. So, when you try to harmonize them, you'll find there's no "room" under the notes for the chords. Before you begin creating your own arrangements, always transpose the melody so that it falls on the first and second strings. That way you'll always have four lower strings for the supporting chords. If you're not sure how to find the same note an octave higher, then you need to refer back to the handy fingerboard diagram on pages 10–11.

Diatonic major chords

Diatonic G major chords (root on top, first inversion)

G   Am   Bm   C   D   Em   F♯dim

Diatonic means "in the key of." In other words a diatonic melody in G major would contain only notes from the G major scale. So, diatonic chords are constructed only from the notes of the parent major scale, in this case G major. If we build a chord on each step of the scale a distinct pattern of major, minor, and diminished chords is established that remains constant in every key. You can use any of these chords to create block harmonizations as illustrated in Exercise 16.2. The diagram above shows the root at the top of the chord (i.e. in first inversion), but you can use any chord note as the melody by using a different inversion.

EXERCISE 16.1

🎧 **Listen to track 27**

This first exercise illustrates the simplest approach to harmonization: adding chords on the beat when the harmony changes (i.e. as indicated by the chord symbols in a lead sheet). The chords can be picked or strummed, but it's important to ensure that they don't overpower the melody notes (which should be played a little harder than the chords).

IMPORTANT TIP

When you're learning a new guitar arrangement, it's a good idea to play the melody on its own first (i.e. notes with stems up, or the top note of block harmonizations as in Exercise 16.2). This will help you to identify the melody so you can play it more expressively when you add the chords. The listener will be able to hear the two parts separately and will be convinced that two guitars are playing.

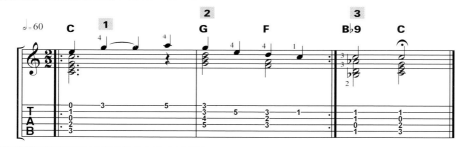

Keep the C chord fretted as you add the high G with your first finger on the second beat. It's important to allow all chords to ring for their full value; this gives the illusion of two guitars playing simultaneously.

Fret the four-note G chord as shown; you don't need to play a full barre shape here. Instead, the first finger forms a semi-barre across the first and second strings. Notice the fourth finger is above the second string ready to add the next melody note, E.

To play the exotic-sounding B♭9 chord, form a barre across the second and third strings with your third finger as shown here. By angling the finger slightly so that it just touches the first string, you can easily mute to avoid obscuring the melody on the second string.

EXERCISE 16.2

🎧 Listen to track 28

In this exercise a much denser harmonic approach is illustrated: where each melody note is harmonized. This technique is called *block harmonization*. To apply this technique successfully you will need to add chords that will not necessarily be given in the lead sheet. The first two bars in this exercise would most likely be harmonized by a single G chord in a songbook. The extra chords are diatonic to the key of G major.

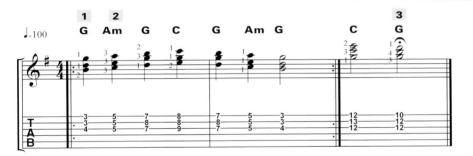

To fret the opening G triad (three-note chord), barre across the first and second strings with your first finger, adding the B on the third string with your second finger as shown here.

To facilitate a quick change to the Am chord on the second beat, simply barre across the top three strings with your third finger. In the second bar (when descending) you'll find that it's easier to use your first finger to barre the same strings.

As you play the final G chord, make sure that your fourth finger is at a 90-degree angle so you can avoid inadvertently muting the melody note on the first string.

EXERCISE 16.3

🎧 **Listen to track 29**
This final exercise mixes both of the previous approaches to harmonization and also introduces the use of double stops in the second bar. Mixing various techniques in this way can produce exciting and dramatic results. Although the notation may look complex, this example is actually quite easy to play.

What is rubato?

Solo guitar pieces are usually played *rubato*, which means "stolen time." When you see this instruction (as in Exercise 16.3), it indicates that you should freely interpret the tempo throughout for dramatic effect. However, always practice the piece with a metronome first and don't slow down just to make the hard bits easier!

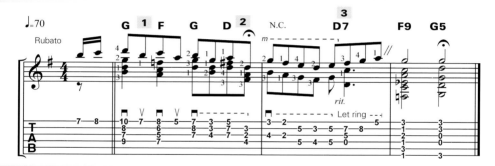

1 Keep the G chord shape fretted when you lift off your fourth finger to play the B on the first beat of bar 1. You then repeat the process two frets lower for the F chord and melody notes.

2 You'll find it's much easier to use down-strums for the triads in the second half of the first bar. Here you can see the final D chord being played with a down-pick. Notice how the pick rests on the first string to ensure it isn't included in the chord.

3 Play the D7 on beat three of the second bar by fretting across the top three strings with a first finger barre as shown here. Keep your finger in position while adding the G and A melody notes because this allows the chord to ring to the end of the bar.

Lesson 17

Moveable chord shapes

Moveable shapes can be played in any key, so they're "must-haves" for the country guitarists' accompaniment toolbox.

There are two types of moveable shapes: barre chords that span five or six strings and non-barre chord shapes that usually involve muting one or two open strings. Both types originated from one of the five basic open shapes in the CAGED system and are illustrated over the next four pages. Barre chords are the most commonly used shapes and are derived from the open E and A chords. The three remaining CAGED shapes, C, G, and D, can also be converted to moveable shapes, either as partial voicings (i.e. without the open-string notes) or with the open strings muted to prevent them from introducing dissonance. Once an open shape has been converted to a moveable one, it can also be played as a minor or dominant seventh chord with very little effort. The barre chords are easiest to locate since the lowest note of the chord is the root note, but start moving partial C, G, or D shapes around and this all changes! Of course, in order to move a chord shape around the neck, you first need to be able to identify and locate the new root note, so any "holes" in your fingerboard knowledge may be highlighted in this process. Make sure your fingerboard geography is up to scratch by referring to the fingerboard map on pages 10–11; this can help you to memorize the names of the notes on every fret. You may already know some of the chord forms featured in this lesson, but don't be tempted to skip it, as it will help you build a practical, working chord vocabulary to assist you on your musical journey.

Where do barre chords come from?

The relationship between the open E chord and the moveable, full six-string barre chord is illustrated here. If you've never played barre chords before, you will find them a little difficult at first. Be patient and practice them frequently (in short bursts) to build up the muscles in your fretting hand.

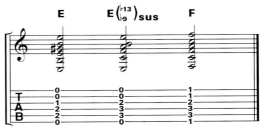

EXAMPLE 1

Barre chord based on open E shape

The chords shown here are all F chords. Move them one fret higher and they become F♯ chords, two frets higher and they're G chords. Easy ain't it? Once you've mastered the major shape, you can easily convert it to the minor or dominant seventh chord shapes shown.

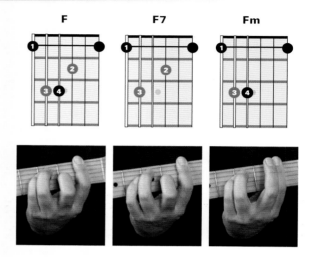

EXAMPLE 2

Barre chord based on open A shape

These shapes are illustrated on the second fret for two reasons: 1) it makes them a little easier to play and 2) you're going to need shapes for B more frequently than B♭ so it makes sense to learn them where you'll be playing them soonest. However, if you find any of these shapes difficult, try moving them further up the neck where less stretching will be required.

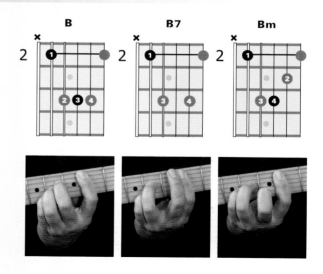

EXAMPLE 3

Moveable chord based on open C shape
The moveable C shape is a tricky shape to memorize because only the dominant seventh variant resembles its open cousin. The major and minor shapes are too awkward to play with the root included, so they're more commonly played as four-note shapes on the top four strings (with the root on the second string).

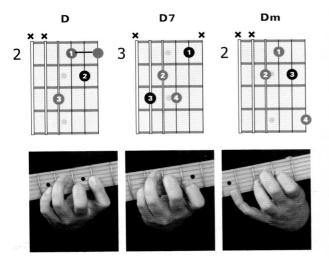

EXAMPLE 4

Moveable chord based on open G shape
Just like the C shape in Example 3 on the previous page, the full open G chord becomes an unwieldy beast when converted to a moveable shape. It's much more practical to play as the four-note shapes shown here. Notice that the root note is now on the third string (R).

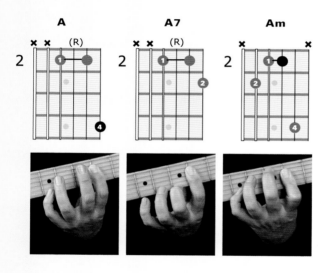

EXAMPLE 5

Moveable chord based on open D shape
Unlike the previous two examples, the full D shape is quite playable when moved up the neck. However, the major variant is commonly played as a three-note chord (by omitting the low root), just as it was in the previous lesson's examples.

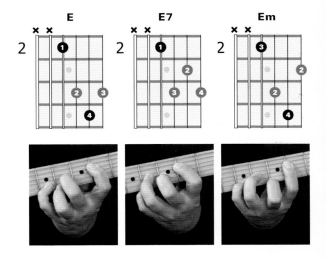

CD

Lesson

18 Cool picking patterns

Learn the fingerpicking techniques of the Nashville session players in this revealing and fun lesson.

What do Dolly Parton, Kenny Rodgers, Johnny Cash, and Alison Krauss all have in common? The answer is that their most famous hits have all featured some deft fingerstyle picking work by Nashville session players. These accompaniments are generally always played on an acoustic, steel-string guitar. Fingerpicked acoustic guitar is synonymous with country music, so it's an essential skill that any aspiring country guitarist simply can't afford to ignore. It's an incredibly versatile technique, too, being equally great for ensemble, duo, or solo accompaniment. There's also nothing more stress-busting than grabbing your acoustic and

pickin' out a few chords after a hard day's work; you'll soon forget all about the day's cares and woes. The exercises in this lesson have been designed to improve your fingerstyle technique. They will give you an insight into the approaches used by the Nashville session men, so they get you one step closer to being the country guitarist you have always dreamed of becoming. Although the exercises may look complex, they only involve using the thumb (*p*) and first two fingers (*i* and *m*) of your picking hand. This makes them quick to learn, so you'll be sounding just like a pro in no time!

IMPORTANT TIP

Spend some time just getting your thumb used to playing alternating bass patterns before you start adding melody notes. The excerpt above is the bassline of Exercise 18.1 with the melody notes removed. Practice each example this way first, only adding melody notes once your thumb is capable of working on "auto pilot."

The chords you'll need for this lesson:

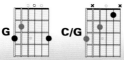

EXERCISE 18.1

🎧 **Listen to track 30**

This first exercise uses a constant picking pattern with only subtle note changes in the second bar. Keeping the chord changes to a minimum allows you to focus on the bassline that alternates between the sixth and fourth strings. Notice that the two repeated melody notes are syncopated and should fall "in the gaps" between the bass notes.

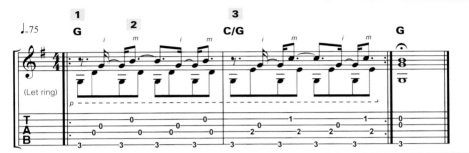

It's very important to keep your picking hand still when you're playing alternating bass patterns. By lightly resting your palm on the bridge you can keep your hand steady and also lightly mute the bass notes to improve the dynamics.

The melody notes should not be picked simultaneously with the bass notes. This would spoil the pattern's syncopated rhythm. Here, you can see that as the second finger (m) picks the second string, the thumb moves across to strike the open D string.

Hold down the chord shapes throughout to allow all the notes to ring into each other. This photograph illustrates how the fretting hand should maintain the full C/G shape throughout bar 2.

F

G7

EXERCISE 18.2

🎧 **Listen to track 31**

This example gives you an opportunity to start using that moveable D7 chord shape from Lesson 17, Example 3. The bassline is a little more complex in this example as it alternates between the fourth, fifth, and sixth strings. Make sure you can play the bassline accurately before you add the melody notes.

To add the low A (the 5th of D7) on the second beat, lift your third finger off the fifth string and onto the sixth (without removing any other fingers from the strings).

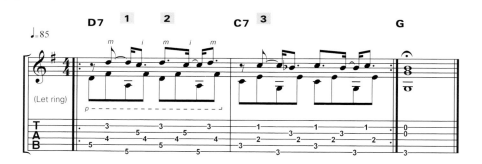

On the third beat, your third finger should return to the fifth string (just before the note is sounded), without removing any other fingers from the strings. This allows the D7 chord notes to ring uninterrupted throughout.

The first melody note of the picking pattern is a pinch, i.e. played simultaneously with the bass note. Here, you can see the thumb (p) striking the fourth string while the first finger (i) picks the second string on the first beat of bar 2.

EXERCISE 18.3

🎧 **Listen to track 32**

This exercise is slightly more challenging than the previous two. Not only does it have a higher "target" tempo, but the melody line is a little more complex. However, you should be finding alternating bass patterns quite natural to play by now, so this will allow you to focus on the syncopated melody.

The pattern begins with a pinch on the first and fifth strings. This photograph shows the notes being correctly played with the thumb and second finger (p and m) of your picking hand.

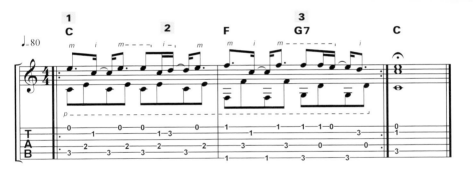

At the end of beat three in the first bar, a D melody note is added with the fourth finger on the third fret. Your remaining fretting-hand fingers should remain in position as shown in this photograph.

In the second bar there's no need to fret the full G7 chord, so the second finger has been omitted from the shape. Notice how the fourth finger should already be hovering in position above the second string as the chord is first sounded on beat three.

CD

Lesson

19

"You Done Me Wrong Again"

This exciting original tune is not only fun to play; it will also help you to hone your newly acquired fingerpicking skills.

For the first time in this book you're going to learn a tune containing both diatonic and non-diatonic chords. We first encountered diatonic chords back in Lesson 16; to recap, a diatonic chord only contains the notes of the parent major scale. Music would sound bland and boring if it only contained diatonic chords. In popular music, songwriters have been "spicing up" their compositions with non-diatonic chords since blues and jazz started to influence popular music in the early 20th century. So country songs will frequently include one or two chords that don't belong in the key of the tune, i.e. non-diatonic chords. These are commonly nothing more dramatic than a minor chord that has been converted to

a dominant seventh, or a major chord that's been turned into a minor. Modulation (a key change) is also frequently used to create harmonic interest and provide a contrast between song sections. So, for instance, in this tune the verse is in D minor but modulates to F major to provide a "lift" in the chorus. So the only non-diatonic chord in this tune is the G7 chord (this includes the variations G, G6, and G/B since they are all functioning as G7). Always analyze chord sequences to identify non-diatonic chords if present. This not only helps you to play licks or solos more effectively, but also helps you to write more interesting chord progressions of your own.

"You Done Me Wrong Again"
Listen to track 33, play with track 34
Although the bass patterns vary slightly, you only need to learn two picking patterns for this arrangement. These are: 1) the verse, with its

repeated one-bar rhythmic pattern and melody notes on the first and second strings and 2) the chorus, which adds rhythmic variation and moves the picking-hand fingers onto the lower second and third strings. It's very

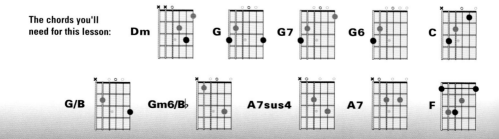

The chords you'll need for this lesson: Dm G G7 G6 C

G/B Gm6/B♭ A7sus4 A7 F

common for country tunes to be based on just one or two picking patterns. This provides a cohesive accompaniment without too much variation that would usurp the vocalist's performance. Reading through (or listening to) an arrangement will help you to become familiar with its structure and to identify variations in the picking patterns before you start work on it.

IMPORTANT TIP

You'll notice that there's a hammer-on at the beginning of the second bar. Fingerpicking hammer-ons are played in exactly the same way as a regular hammer-on; pick only the first note and then quickly "hammer" your finger onto the string to sound the second. Adding slurs to fingerpicking patterns is a cool way to add extra notes without changing the picking pattern.

Dm

* Hammer-on played
open to first fret
using the first finger.

Be a better player

As a golden rule, always learn the bass part first! You'll never achieve satisfactory results unless you physically separate the bassline from the melody, learning it independently. Take your time; you'll only be ready to move onto the melody once you can play the bassline on "auto pilot." Next make sure that you understand exactly where each melody note falls rhythmically. Is it a pinch (played with a bass note) or syncopated (played between the bass notes)? Add the melody notes to your bassline gradually, starting with the first note and only adding successive notes once you can loop each bar three times without error. It goes without saying that you should attempt no more than a few bars in each practice session. This may seem pedantic but it really is the quickest and most accurate way to learn; it's a tried-and-tested approach that banishes mistakes, bad habits, and frustration from the get-go.

G7   Bb   C7   A7sus4   A7

You Done Me Wrong Again

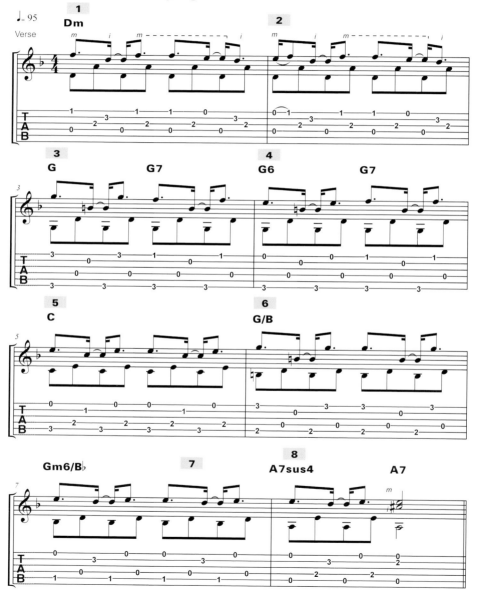

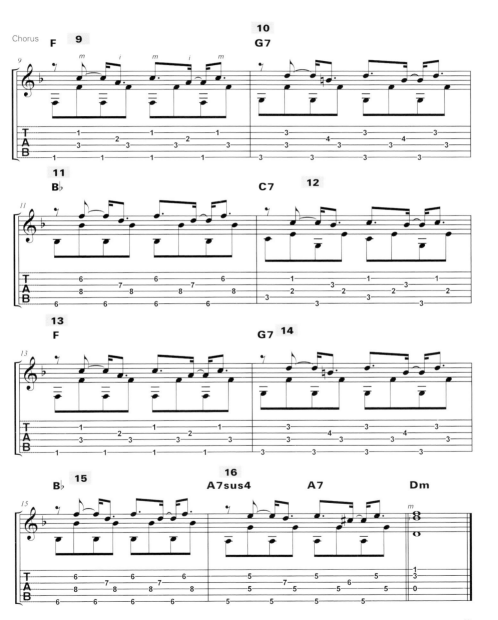

Continue for step by steps ▶▶

Bar 1 beat 1 *This photograph clearly illustrates how the thumb and second finger (p and m) should be positioned in order to play the pinch on the first beat of bar 1.*

Bar 2 beat 1 *To execute the hammer-on at the start of bar 2, first lift your first finger off the string, as shown here. Make sure that your fourth finger is clear of the string or the note will not sound.*

Bar 3 beat 1 *Make sure you fret the G chord in bar 3 using your third and fourth fingers as shown here. Notice that because the fifth string is not picked, there is no need to fret it; your second finger can remain hovering above the strings.*

Bar 4 beat 1 *To play the G6 chord in bar 4, you only need to fret the low G bass note as shown here. The remaining notes are all picked from open strings.*

IMPORTANT TIP

When faced with the prospect of learning "chord-heavy" arrangements like this one, you'll find it's a great help to just strum through the arrangement a few times. This will help you to learn the chord shapes and memorize the sequence more quickly, leaving you free to concentrate on your picking hand.

Bar 5 beat 1 Hold down the full C chord shape throughout bar 5. This ensures that all of the notes are allowed to ring into each other.

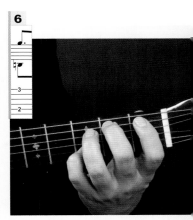

Bar 6 beat 1 Fret the G/B chord using your second and fourth fretting-hand fingers. Notice how the first finger is already in position above the first fret ready to play the low Bb that follows in bar 7.

Bar 7 beat 3 Your thumb should continue to alternate between the fourth and fifth strings in bar 7. Here you can see it in action, picking the fourth string while the first finger (i) prepares to play the second string on beat three.

Bar 8 beat 1 While keeping your fourth finger in position on the second string, remove your first finger and add your second finger on the fourth fret. This allows you to make a quick change to the A7sus4 chord.

9

Bar 9 beat 1 *For the chorus section, your first and second picking-hand fingers move on to the lower melody strings. Here you can see the second finger (m) correctly picking the second string in bar 9 while the thumb (p) simultaneously picks the fourth string.*

10

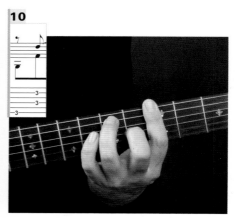

Bar 10 beat 1 *It's important to ensure that your first finger is making good contact with all six strings when fretting the full G7 barre. If it isn't, the bass note on the fourth string may not ring clearly.*

11

Bar 11 beat 1 *Playing the full B♭ barre chord involves a quick position shift from the third to the sixth fret shown here. Don't take your fingers off the strings when moving. Just release your fretting-hand pressure and slide the shape along the strings.*

12

Bar 12 beat 1 *The bass pattern changes in bar 12, alternating between all three bass strings instead of just two. This photograph captures the thumb just after playing the E on beat one. Notice that it needs to jump right over the fifth string to play the sixth string.*

13

Bar 13 beat 1 *It's sometimes tricky to get all of the notes of the full F barre to ring clearly. Keeping your first finger parallel to the first fret and snugly behind it will help you produce clearer notes.*

14

Bar 14 beat 1 *As soon as your thumb has played the first low G bass note in bar 14, it should immediately move toward the fourth string (by jumping over the fifth) to play the D bass note that quickly follows.*

15

Bar 15 beat 3 *Don't forget that your second finger (m) should be picking the second string throughout the chorus section. This photograph illustrates the pinch on the first beat of bar 15 with the thumb simultaneously playing the fourth string.*

16

Bar 16 beat 3 *As you fret the A7sus4 barre chord in the penultimate bar, place your second finger on the third string as shown here. This will enable you to change smoothly to the A7 chord by simply lifting your fourth finger off the third string.*

CD

Lesson

20 Swing grooves

Learn how to jazz-up your country playing with Western-swing-style riffs and licks.

Just as blues and rock music can be played with either a straight or a shuffle feel, the same groove variations are also used in country music. However, in country, the swing groove has more to do with the influence of jazz, and specifically big band jazz, during the 1930s and 40s. Western swing, as its name implies, was country music's take on the popular swing music of the day. Often played at faster tempos, it was the first sub-genre of country music that allowed the musicians to "show off" and display their virtuosity. It was during this period that the pedal steel guitar first started to feature in line-ups; with instrumental tunes such as Leon McAuliffe's "Steel Guitar Rag" (1936) becoming popular

additions to many bands' repertoires. The swing groove is still widely used in today's country music, but without the horn arrangements that were a big feature of the Western swing genre in its heyday. Contemporary Western swing is no longer the preserve of the slide guitarist either; virtuoso players like Brad Paisley and Brent Mason often add up-tempo swing tracks to their repertoire to provide a vehicle for a bit of country shredding. The swing groove is now such an important part of mainstream country music that you simply can't afford to ignore it. As Duke Ellington's most famous tune says in it's title, "It don't mean a thing, if it ain't got that swing!"

The roots of Western swing

The roots of Western swing date back to the 1920s and the swing bands of Western and Southern USA. The band members were country musicians who were influenced by the rise in popularity of swing jazz during the period. It's worth remembering that jazz was the popular music in the USA at this time; country music was still in its infancy. During the 1930s and 40s, Western swing bands were incredibly popular, especially in Texas, Oklahoma, and California. The big stars of the period included Bob Wills and the Texas Playboys, Milton Brown and His Musical Brownies, and the wonderfully named The Light Crust Doughboys.

The chords you'll need for this lesson:

 F

 C

 G

 E9

EXERCISE 20.1

Listen to track 35

This simple, arpeggio-based accompaniment figure is perfect for medium-tempo swing grooves. Don't forget that swing tunes are always written with "straight" eighth notes; only the "swing" instruction beneath the tempo marking will inform you of the correct interpretation.

It's important to hold down the full chord shapes throughout to allow all the notes to ring clearly. Notice that the F chord shape used here is the smaller, four-note type, and not the full six-string barre.

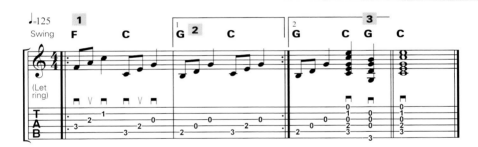

Use the alternate picking as indicated, keeping your pick constantly moving even when the up-picks are not played. This photograph illustrates the fourth string correctly played with an up-pick on the first beat of bar 2.

To facilitate a quick chord change, you can play the G chord by fretting only the sixth string with your third finger as shown here. Angle the finger gently onto the fifth string to prevent it from sounding.

EXERCISE 20.2

🎧 **Listen to track 36**

When you're playing swing grooves, it's more than likely that you will encounter eighth-note triplets. These can be tricky to pick correctly because they disrupt the usual "down-up" pattern of alternate eighth-note picking. This exercise illustrates how you can use a combination of slides and economy picking to get round the issue and make your performance sound slick and professional.

Fret the low G on beat two with your third finger. As you slide the note up to G♯ your hand will move to second position (first finger on the second fret) where the riff is easier to play.

Fret the D on the fifth string at the start of beat three using your fourth finger as shown here. If you use your third finger you will move out of position and be unable to fret the B that then follows.

The F♯ on beat three of bar 2 should be fretted with your third finger. Keep it pressed down as you play the open G that follows, allowing the two notes to briefly ring into each other.

EXERCISE 20.3

🎧 **Listen to track 37**

This up-tempo swing lick can be used in many different scenarios; it's perfect as a fill, an ending, or as part of a full solo. It's got all of the classic country hallmarks, including an iconic Duane Eddy-esque half-step bend that rounds off the phrase nicely. Notice that slides are used to alleviate any awkward picking during the opening triplets.

IMPORTANT TIP

A swing feel is only ever indicated by the instruction "swing" or "shuffle" at the start of a piece of music. It is never actually written rhythmically. How much or how little swing is applied is down to the individual player; it's part of what makes every country player sound different. When you're first getting the groove together, think of swing eighth notes as the first and third beats in a group of three eighth-note triplets:

The slide from C♯ to D should be played with your third finger. Keep the note fretted as you play the E with your first finger to allow the two notes to ring into each other.

Fret the G♯ grace note on beat three with your third finger. As you slide down to the F♯ your hand will move to second position (i.e. first finger on the second fret) where you can comfortably play the remaining notes.

The sixth string is quite hard to bend, especially low on the neck. So, by using your second finger to fret the low F♯, you can add the first finger behind it for extra strength when bending, as shown here.

CD

tracks 38, 39

Lesson

21 "Texas Shuffle"

This tune's hotter than a Texan barbecue in July, so grab your guitar and get ready to start smokin'.

You just can't beat an up-tempo shuffle groove for getting feet a-tappin' and folks into a party mood! And that's just what this tune is all about: having some fun while you put your new chops into practice. Contemporary country shuffle tunes tend to display a wider range of influences than the original Western swing style. This is primarily due to the huge influence that the electric guitar has had on popular music. So, modern country shuffle riffs tend to be more blues-based; the heavy jazz influence having become less prominent. The guitar tones have also shifted toward a more rock-orientated sound in recent decades with crunchy, overdriven tones becoming the order of the day. That aside, the groove remains the same; that infectious rhythm which made the original Western swing bands so popular is just as hot and swingin' today as it was back in the 1940s.

"Texas Shuffle"
Listen to track 38, play with track 39
The most important thing to do before you start learning this tune is to get used to thinking in triplets; this helps you to get that shuffle groove internalized from the get-go. Although the drummer is clearly playing a shuffle groove on the backing track, your playing will sound stronger and sit more "in the pocket" if you take a little time to focus on the groove during your warm-up. Of course, the more shuffle and swing grooves you play, the more experienced you'll become and the less you'll need to do this. For now, however, it's important to make sure you're really feeling that shuffle correctly. Start by setting your metronome below the tempo of the track (100 bpm is a good starting-point), and tap out the beat using two hands. You can accent the

Unison slides

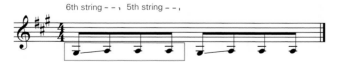

Unison slides are frequently used in riffs, fills, and licks, so it's important to play them correctly or you won't achieve that iconic country sound! By repeating a fretted note on an open string, the subtle difference in timbre and tuning creates a unique texture; sliding a half step into the first note enhances this effect. However, it's important to allow the first note to ring for its full written value (in this case an eighth note) before you slide.

groups of triplets by emphasizing them first with your right hand and then with your left (RIGHT-left-right LEFT-right-left etc.). Once you're comfortable with this, you can then remove the middle note to leave correctly swinging eighth notes. If you want to take the idea further, why not try switching directly between straight and swing eighths? Remember that rhythm is the single most important element of music, so it's really important to make sure you're playing (and feeling) it right.

Be a better player

Rhythmic vs. grace-note bends

Although you've already played grace-note and rhythmic bends in earlier lessons, it won't do any harm to take another look at how to execute them both correctly. Rhythmic accuracy is especially important when grace-note and rhythmic bends feature in the same phrase, as they do in this tune. The example below illustrates how to practice a phrase containing both types of bend by first omitting them. By doing this you can ensure that you're not side-tracked by the string bending; you can hear exactly how the phrase should sound. When you add the bends back in you'll be able to give the correct rhythmic weighting to both the grace note and the rhythmic bends.

Remember that a grace-note bend should have no rhythmic duration; it's just a starting-point. Simply play the note and bend it immediately to the pitch as indicated in the notation or TAB. Rhythmic bends should be treated differently: the first note should be allowed to ring for the duration indicated before you bend it or release it.

Bar 4 with bends removed   **Bar 4 with bends**

Texas Shuffle

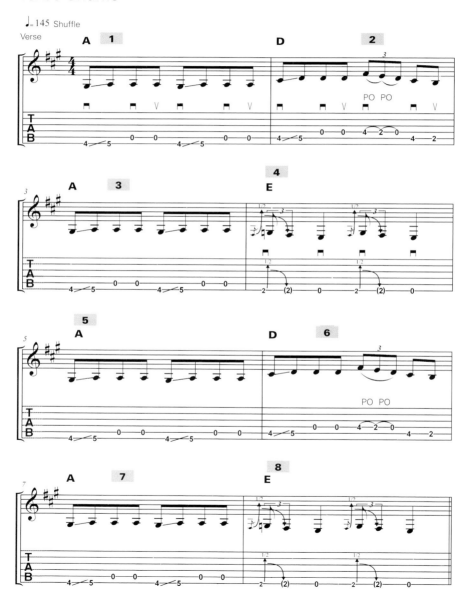

Chorus

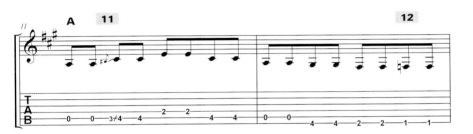

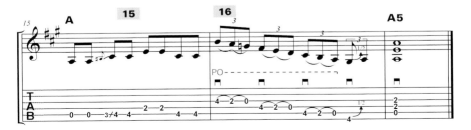

Continue for step by steps ▶▶

Bar 1 beat 1 *Eighth-note alternate picking should be used throughout, ghosting your pick upward to maintain the rhythm on the off-beat (this is where you slide into the G♯ so that the note is not picked).*

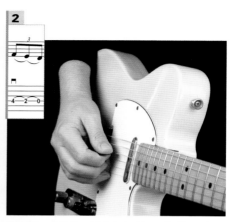

Bar 2 beat 3 *The triplet double pull-off on the third beat should be played with a strong down-pick as shown here. Remember that you don't need to pick the two notes that follow; the pitches are generated by releasing your fretting fingers with a sideways motion.*

Bar 3 beat 2 *As you pick the two open A notes on the second beat, move your third finger back to the fourth fret ready to play the G♯ on beat three.*

Bar 4 beat 1 *Use down-picks to play the bends on the first and third beats. This will produce a strong, clear note, enabling you to bend the string and release it again without re-picking it.*

Bar 5 beat 1 *Fret the G♯ with your third finger, sliding up to the fifth fret without re-picking. Allow the fretted A to ring briefly into the open A, taking care to ensure that your third finger is not inadvertently damping the fifth string.*

Bar 6 beat 2 *As you're playing the open fourth string on beat two, move your hand back down to second position so that your third finger is in position above the fourth fret as shown here.*

Bar 7 beat 2 *Try to maintain a good fretting-hand position at all times. Here you can clearly see the third finger in position above the fourth fret, with the remaining fingers nice and close to the fingerboard.*

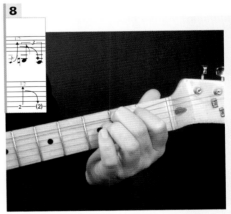

Bar 8 beat 1 *Don't try to bend that low sixth string with just one finger! Use two fingers (you can even use three if you'd prefer) as shown here.*

Bar 9 beat 2 *Unlike the verse section, the slide on beat two of the opening chorus bar is a grace-note slide. As soon as you've picked the note, slide your third finger straight up to the fourth fret.*

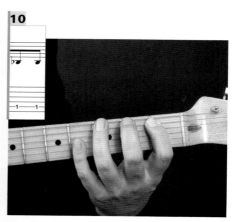

Bar 10 beat 4 *Use your first finger to play the B♭ at the end of bar 10. This will move your hand into first position and ready to...*

Bar 11 beat 2 *...play the B♯ on the third fret with your third finger. Remember to keep your finger pressed firmly onto the fret as you slide or you will not hear the second note.*

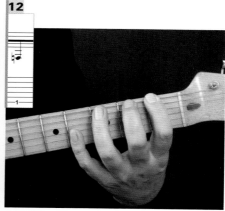

Bar 12 beat 4 *The same process should be applied to beat four of bar 13: i.e. play the low F on the first fret using your first finger. This simultaneously moves your hand into first position ready for the notes that follow.*

Bar 13 beat 1 *Keep your hand in first position as you pick the two open E notes at the start of bar 13. Your third finger should hover above the third fret, perfectly positioned to play the slide into the G♯.*

Bar 14 beat 2 *There's quite a tricky bend release on the second beat of this bar. As soon as you've released the bend, quickly move your first finger onto the second fret ready for the pull-off that follows.*

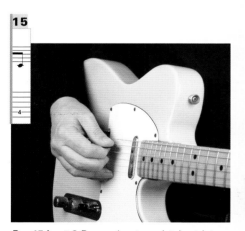

Bar 15 beat 2 *Remember to maintain strict alternate picking throughout. This photograph shows the pick correctly playing the second C♯ on beat two with an up-pick.*

Bar 16 beat 1 *The concluding lick is based on a descending series of double pull-offs, so it's very important to get that sideways finger release just right. By moving your thumb to the edge of the neck you can change your hand position slightly to facilitate this.*

CD

Lesson

22

Open tunings for slide

Discover the legacy of the Mississippi Delta bluesmen who
played slide by tuning their guitars to a chord.

There's no denying that the blues had an
enormous influence on every guitar-based
genre that followed in its wake. So it's no
surprise that the country guitar pioneers drew
inspiration from the blues guitarists of the day,
especially the bottleneck blues players. The
bluegrass slide pioneers borrowed the open
tunings of the bluesmen, turned their guitars
face-upward, and played them on their laps.
Lap-style slide guitar requires a specialty
instrument with a fat, square neck; it isn't the
remit of this book to delve into such a specialty
niche, so the exercises and tunes that follow
this lesson can all be played on a regular guitar,
played in the conventional way. This is actually
how the majority of contemporary electric
players play country slide today. However, if
you find yourself diggin' slide in a big way, you
may want to go the whole hog and explore the
more traditional route with a lap guitar.
Whichever path you choose, you'll find that the
following lessons will give you a valuable
insight into the tips and tricks of the country
slide guitarist.

IMPORTANT TIP

Don't forget that if you're using an
electronic tuner, make sure that your
guitar's volume is turned up full. When
you're tuning an acoustic guitar, rest the
tuner on your leg in order to keep the
built-in mic as close to the soundhole
as possible. See Lesson 4, pages 22—23.

Setting up your guitar for slide

Before we delve into the mechanics of open
tunings it's worth mentioning that slide
technique is easier on a guitar with heavy
strings and a high action. If you get into slide in
a big way, you'll probably want to invest in a
separate guitar that you can set up just for this
purpose, but it's not essential. Resonator
acoustics are ideal for slide playing; they
provide an authentic country sound and, since
most acoustics come with fairly heavy, factory-
fitted strings, they require little, if any, setting
up. It's the electric guitar that is more
problematic for slide players. The light strings
and lower action mean that, without being
specifically set up for slide, your bottleneck will
constantly be making a horrible sound as it
runs aground on the frets.

Open tunings

There are many open tunings that can be used
for playing slide. To keep things simple we'll be
focusing on the two most popular open
tunings: G and D. The point of tuning to a chord
instead of sticking with regular tuning is that it
allows a major chord to be played by simply
laying the slide across the strings. You can't
add fingers in front of the slide to form chords
as you can with regular guitar technique.

To help you get in tune, we've included tuning
notes on the accompanying CD. Each string is
played three times, in order to give you plenty
of time to tune.

OPEN G TUNING

🎧 **Listen to track 40**

This widely used tuning is also very popular with blues and rock musicians, most notably Keith Richards of the Rolling Stones who has played almost exclusively in this tuning since the late 1960s. It's the easiest open tuning to get to grips with because the second, third, and fourth strings remain unchanged; this keeps the essential "home" notes of your pentatonic scales in the same location. To tune to open G, the first, fifth, and sixth strings are all lowered a whole step (one tone). Check the open G against the third string, and the first and sixth strings against the fourth string. Most good tuners will have no problem recognizing the lower pitches.

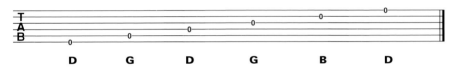

D   G   D   G   B   D

OPEN D TUNING

🎧 **Listen to track 41**

This deep, full open tuning will really make your guitar resonate! It's a little more complex than open G to get your head around at first, but once you do you'll find it's an extremely logical open tuning to use for slide. To tune to open D you'll need to change the pitch of four strings. The first, second, and sixth strings should be lowered a whole step, while the third string is lowered just a half step (semitone). Check the open second string against the fifth string, and the first and sixth strings against the fourth string. Again, a good-quality tuner will have no problem recognizing these notes, and may already have presets for open tunings.

D   A   D   F♯   A   D

Lesson

23 Slide guitar techniques

Learn how to play accurate slide guitar and stop your dog from howlin' everytime you pick up that guitar.

Slide guitar is one of the most expressive of all guitar techniques. It's an extremely haunting sound, primarily because it sounds so similar to a human voice. The absence of frets means that you can slide in and out of notes and really make that guitar "talk." Unfortunately, that same absence of frets can make your first experience of playing slide rather painful, and not just for the other humans that share your

life! The old slide player's advice to the novice is a harsh reminder of how bad slide can sound, "Son, when your dog stops howlin', then you know you're startin' to get better!" However, things needn't be too painful if you take heed of the essential tips and tricks revealed in this invaluable lesson.

TECHNIQUE 1

Play in tune
The first thing that needs to be addressed when playing slide is how to play a note that's in tune. When we fret a note conventionally, we're placing our finger behind the fret; it's actually the fret that's making the note. So, if you place your slide where your finger would be, the resulting note would actually sound flat. So the first thing is to get used to playing over the frets and not behind them. It's one of those simple tips that seems obvious once it's been pointed out, and it's guaranteed to improve your slide playing 100%. The photograph to the right shows exactly how your slide should look when you're playing it in the correct position, right above the fret.

Keep your thumb in position behind the neck and make sure your slide is placed over the fret, not behind it where your finger would normally fret.

TECHNIQUE 2

Damp those strings

When you're playing single-string slide licks, it's not possible to press the slide down on individual strings; it's going to be lying across several strings at once. So, as soon as you pick another string, the previous one is going to keep ringing. In fact, all six strings are going to be making a sound, generated by the friction of the bottleneck on the strings. You need to get used to damping all of the un-played strings all of the time. There are two ways of damping, and both should be used simultaneously. You can't rely on just one if you want to sound like the pros.

The first technique is very simple, as shown in the left photograph below. If you're wearing the slide on your third finger (and this is the best finger to wear it on), then rest your first and second fingers on the strings behind it. This effectively damps notes *behind* the slide, removing unwanted noise that will be generated by its movement along the strings.

The second technique is a little more complex and involves damping the strings in front of the slide. It's this technique that you use to stop notes from ringing into each other when playing across the strings, or reducing string noise generated by the slide when playing along a single string. To mute the lower strings you can rest your palm on the strings close to the bridge, but you'll find that it's more effective to use a combination of economical slide placement (i.e. laying it across as few strings as possible) and direct string damping using your second and third fingers (*m* and *a*). The fingers can be rested on any adjacent strings that are not being played. Because you will need to move on and off the strings as they are played, this involves a high degree of coordination, so it can be tricky to master. However, like all the other techniques covered in this book, it can be built slowly as you work through the exercises in the lessons that follow.

Here you can see the first and second fingers laying on the string behind the slide, damping unwanted harmonics that will be generated as the slide moves along the strings.

Rest the palm of your picking hand on the lower strings to mute unwanted bass notes. Notice how the second and third fingers (m and a) are also resting on the upper strings to mute them.

TECHNIQUE 3

Use vibrato—sparingly

Vibrato shouldn't be overdone when you're learning how to pitch notes accurately. It can obscure the fact that you're not quite "on" the note. It's also fatiguing to listen to when overdone. That said, vibrato is a very important part of slide technique. It is more expressive than regular guitar vibrato because you can slip below the note as well as above it just like a singer. When you're playing notes with your fingers, this can only be used when string bending. To play vibrato effectively, start with your slide right above the fret and gradually introduce vibrato by moving the slide quickly up and down the strings (not too far, just a few millimeters in each direction).

This photograph shows vibrato being added to a chord on the fifth fret—notice that the slide has traveled in front of the fret...

...and then just behind the fifth fret. A constant, smooth alternation between these two positions will produce a pleasing vibrato.

IMPORTANT TIP

To avoid having to mute all of the strings that you're not playing, don't lay your slide across all six strings at once. Many players also lift the slide off the higher strings and angle it onto the lower strings to prevent the top strings resonating on low riffs.

*Dedicate some time to practicing the
three core techniques outlined in
this lesson and you'll soon get the
hang of playing slide guitar.*

CD

Lesson

24 Open G pentatonic scales

In this lesson you'll learn how to play two essential country scales in open G tuning.

You should, by now, be quite familiar with the sound of the major pentatonic and major blues pentatonic scales. Having the sound of a scale "in your head" will help you to play these scales more accurately when you're learning them in open tunings. The familiar standard tuning patterns will have changed dramatically, so knowing how the scale should sound is really essential, particularly as you have to "make" each note with the slide. That's one of the hardest things about slide guitar: just like a violin, there are no frets to generate perfectly in-tune notes; you have to do that yourself.

That's why learning scale patterns before you try and play any licks is crucial. Don't forget you'll also need to use all of the techniques discussed in the previous lesson too: behind-the-fret string damping, using your picking hand palm and fingers to mute the strings, and making sure you're always playing directly over the fret and not behind it. So, don't be in too much of a hurry to get onto the next lesson, take your time, play these exercises slowly, and you'll avoid upsetting that country bloodhound out on the porch!

Interval checker

You should by now be familiar with the construction of the major pentatonic and major blues scales since these were covered back in Lesson 10. However, in this lesson we'll be transposing the scales into C major, so, although the interval construction remains the same, the names of the notes will be different as you can see below:

Major pentatonic

R   2   3   5   6   Oct

Major blues pentatonic

R   2   ♯2/♭3   3   5   6   Oct

The chord you'll
need for this lesson:

C

EXERCISE 24.1

🎧 **Listen to track 42**

The CAGED system is less relevant when playing slide. That's because you can't play five different shapes without using your fingers. So, the slide approach is either horizontal i.e. along the string, or vertical i.e. across the strings. When playing across the strings, visualizing the root-position chord shape helps to locate the essential notes. To play a C major chord, lay your slide across the fifth fret, making sure that the slide is parallel and directly above the fret. The lowest note has been bracketed because it is not the root note; it's the fifth of the chord. However, by starting your strum on the fifth string you can easily omit it.

IMPORTANT TIP

It's really important to play these exercises slowly. There's absolutely nothing to be gained (and everything to be lost) from rushing. In fact, 60 bpm is probably going to be too quick the first time you play them, so try playing a note every two beats to begin with. Remember that speed is not the object of each exercise; it's all about generating "in tune" and clearly audible notes.

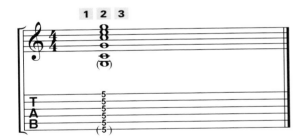

Make sure that your slide is parallel with the fret.

Keep your slide above the fret, not behind it.

Start your strum from the fifth string, sweeping your pick smoothly and evenly across the remaining strings.

EXERCISE 24.2

🎧 **Listen to track 43**

This is the C major pentatonic scale with its root note on the fifth string. Notice how all of the essential chord tones (R-3-5) fall on the fifth fret (C chord shape). Visualizing the C chord shape while you're playing the scale will help you to learn the pattern quicker; it will also help you to locate the essential chord notes when improvising licks. As always, you should practice the scale ascending and descending.

Always remember to lay two fingers across the strings behind the slide. This will mute any unwanted harmonics, helping you to produce a cleaner sound.

Before sliding up to the second note on the seventh fret, mute the string by placing your pick back onto the string as shown here. It's a good idea to make this your default picking approach for slide.

Unplayed higher strings can be muted by keeping your fingers resting on them as shown in this photograph.

EXERCISE 24.3

🎧 **Listen to track 44**
This example adds the "blue" note (D♯) to
generate the major pentatonic blues scale.
To add this note, you will need to move
the slide in smaller increments (half steps)
than before, so don't forget to keep
checking that it's resting directly on top of
the relevant fret and not behind it.

*Always remember to damp the string before
you move the slide to a new note. This
photograph shows the pick resting on the
string just before the slide moves up to the
seventh fret.*

*Ensure that your slide remains parallel to the
frets at all times. This photograph illustrates
the D♯ on beat three, correctly played with the
slide directly above the eighth fret.*

*As you move onto the top strings, you can
reposition the slide so that only the tip of it
makes contact with the first and second
strings as shown here. Doing this means you'll
only need to mute the string you're not playing.*

CD

Lesson

25 Open G slide licks

Now that you've got your slide technique happening, it's time to learn some cool licks!

In this lesson you'll be learning three pentatonic licks to kick-start your lick library. As you get deeper into the world of slide guitar, you should think about transcribing the licks of the great players. Don't attempt whole solos; it's much better to just work out short licks that you can start using right away. Even in the age of technology and instant information, nothing beats the tried-and-tested method of transcribing for getting your chops together. Transcribing improves your aural skills, builds your vocabulary, and provides a constant source of inspiration. Always do your research, though, and check

what tuning a player uses before you start. There's nothing worse than spending hours struggling with a lick only to find out that you're in the wrong tuning. Just as you did when you played the scales in the previous lesson, it's important to remember to incorporate all of your slide skills when you're working on these exercises. Pay attention to your pitching and string damping in particular. Remember that playing slide guitar is not easy, but be patient and you'll soon be astounding your friends with your supercool slide work!

Open G major pentatonic

Transposing the C major scale pattern from Lesson 24 is very easy; simply move the shape to the fret that has the corresponding root note on the fifth string.
In Exercise 25.1 the scale is transposed to open position to include as many open strings as possible. This changes the pattern slightly because you can no longer play notes "behind" the chord shape:

The chord you'll need for this lesson:

EXERCISE 25.1

🎧 **Listen to track 45**

If this cool open G lick doesn't give you the slide "bug," then nothing will! It's "low down 'n' mean" and could be used in several different musical contexts: as a song ending, as an intro, or even a song's main riff. Just change a couple of notes here and there to make it your own.

IMPORTANT TIP

To make sure you're positioning the slide correctly and producing nicely "in-tune" notes, try playing each lick without the slide first. You can always omit any slides between notes if you're wrestling with a high-action guitar set up for slide. Doing this will help you to hear exactly how each note should sound when played correctly.

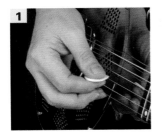

In this photograph you can see the third finger (a) has been placed on the first string to damp it as the pick moves over to play the A♯ on the third string. Because the note is marked as staccato, you need to damp it immediately after playing it.

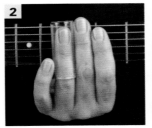

Slide into the A on the third beat from the B♭ on the third fret. Notice how the slide is placed directly above the third fret in order to produce the correct pitch.

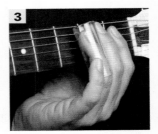

By angling your slide "into" the fifth string you should be able to lift it clear of the higher strings as shown here. This will reduce the number of strings you need to damp with your picking hand.

EXERCISE 25.2

🎧 **Listen to track 46**

This lick returns to the key of C major and the major pentatonic shape based around the C major chord on the fifth fret. Notice the use of the open string on the second beat. Although this note could have been played on the fourth string, it gives the opening phrase an authentic sound by keeping all the notes on the same string (i.e. a horizontal approach).

To avoid having to damp all six strings when you're just playing one string, the slide can be positioned so that it covers only the top four strings as shown here.

Keep the first and second strings muted by resting your (m) and (a) fingers on them throughout the first bar. Notice that the palm is also resting on the fifth and sixth strings.

Slide into the final C from the third fret. This is a grace-note slide, so remember to move the slide up to the fifth fret immediately after you've picked the note.

EXERCISE 25.3

🎧 **Listen to track 47**

This lick is a little more demanding than the previous examples because it not only spans five strings, but also incorporates a half-step slide into the final C major chord. Finishing your lick on a chord is a cool thing to do; it will provide an effective conclusion to any phrase.

This photograph illustrates the (m) finger damping the first string as soon as the slide has arrived at the fifth fret to keep it short. Notice that the pick is already above the second string ready to play the next note.

As you slide up from the fifth fret to the seventh on beat four, ensure that your first and second fingers continue to damp the strings behind the slide as shown here.

When you're playing the half-step slide into the final C chord, make sure that the slide remains parallel with the frets throughout or the resulting chord will sound out of tune.

CD

Lesson

26 "Cajun Sunrise"

This original tune has a strong melody, so you can play it with or without the backing track.

Some tunes just don't work without accompaniment; they need a supporting riff or groove to make them sound good. Other tunes are so strong that they sound complete without any accompaniment at all. It's the second category of tune that guitar players seek out as a repertoire for solo performance. And the slide guitarist also has a distinct advantage when it comes to playing solo. For starters, that haunting, almost primeval sound instantly hooks in the listener because it sounds so close to the human voice. Secondly, because the slide guitar is tuned to a chord, it's easier to add supporting harmony to a melody. For the best results, play along with the backing track first. This will ensure that you get the pitching spot-on and the phrasing in time. Then, once you've got the tune down, try playing it solo. To get the vibe right, you can imagine you're out on the range, pickin' out a lonely slide melody as the sun comes up and the coffee brews over the fire.

"Cajun Sunrise"
Listen to track 48, play with track 49
This song may sound relaxed and laid back, but that doesn't necessarily mean it's going to be easy! Remember that good musicians should be able to fool the listener into thinking that the music is flowing effortlessly from their fingers. The tempo of this tune is quite bright (125 bpm), especially once you figure in all that string damping that will be needed between those eighth notes. So, as always, start with a short, manageable section and practice it slowly until you can play it without mistakes. As a rule of thumb, once you can play a section correctly three times (consecutively), then you've nailed it. It's no good playing something over and over, and then stopping when you finally play it right. If the last time you played it was the only correct version, you could have 20 incorrect attempts stored in your muscle memory. Practice is unquestionably all about repetition, but it's also about repeating correctly, without mistakes. That's the secret of efficient practicing.

The chords you'll need for this lesson:

 C   5

 D   7

 F   10

 G

Be a better player

Get those notes and chords in tune!

We've already compared the slide guitar to the violin because it doesn't make the note for you; you need to rely on your ear to tell you when you're playing in tune. But, actually, violin players have an even tougher time because they have no visual indicators to help them (slide guitars still have frets and position markers). So, make good use of this advantage and keep checking that your slide is directly above the fret and not behind it, using your ear as the final confirmation of accuracy. You can practice your listening skills by playing slide chords along with a loop, backing track, or by jamming with a friend. The idea is to match a simple sequence of major chords on regular guitar with the slide. Don't slide into the chords at first; just see if you can play them in tune straight off. Try doing this with the backing track for this tune and hitting just the chord at the start of each bar. This can be varied by playing all six strings or just two or three, and also by playing the G chord at the twelfth fret (open G is too easy!).

Experiment by playing partial chords as well as full six-string voicings. Here you can see only the top four strings are being played.

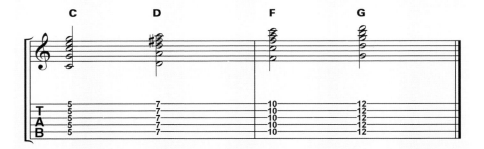

"Cajun Sunrise"

Open G tuning (DGDGBD)

Continue for step by steps ▸▸

Bar 1 beat 1 *As your pick returns to play the G with an up-pick, allow the side of your thumb to make contact with the second string and damp it. This prevents the first note from ringing into the second.*

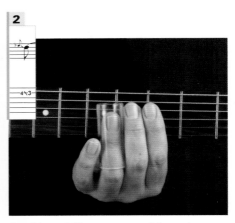

Bar 2 beat 2 *The grace-note slide on the second beat of bar 2 is a half-step that descends from the fourth to the third fret. Keep your slide directly above the fret as shown here.*

Bar 3 beat 3 *Keep the first and second strings muted throughout the C-B-C slide on the third beat by resting your (m) and (a) fingers on the strings as shown here.*

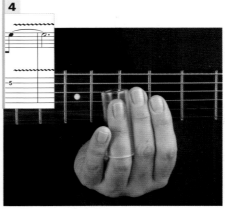

Bar 4 beat 1 *Add vibrato to the long C note by oscillating the slide lengthwise along the string. Be careful that you don't drift off pitch; don't forget that your "home" position is directly above the fifth fret as shown here.*

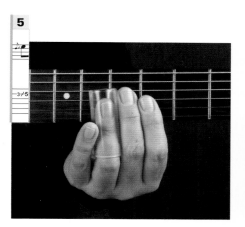

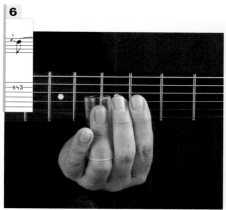

Bar 5 beat 1 *As you slide from the D to the E on the first beat, make sure your bottleneck doesn't overshoot its target. You should finish with the slide directly above the fifth fret as illustrated here.*

Bar 6 beat 2 *The grace-note slide in this bar starts a fret higher than it did in bar 2 to provide contrast and variation. Make sure that your slide is positioned on the fifth fret as illustrated here before you pick the string.*

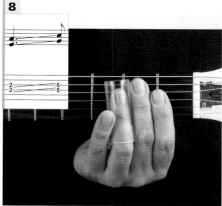

Bar 7 beat 1 *By using your pick and second finger (m), you can easily hybrid pick the double stop on the first beat of bar 7 as shown in this photograph.*

Bar 8 beat 3 *At the end of bar 8, a slow slide starts on the second fret and ascends to the fifth. Move the slide slowly, ensuring that the slide remains parallel to the frets and in contact with the strings throughout.*

Bar 9 beat 4 *As soon as you've picked the last note in bar 9, rest the side of your thumb briefly on the string to damp it. This prevents an unwanted slide from sounding as you move up to the seventh fret.*

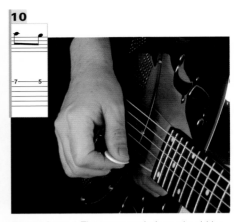

Bar 10 beat 1 *The same technique should be applied at the beginning of bar 10. Before moving your slide back down to the fifth fret, damp the string with the side of your thumb.*

Bar 11 beat 1 *Because the notes on the first beat should be allowed to ring into each other, it's very important to keep your slide parallel to the frets to avoid out-of-tune notes.*

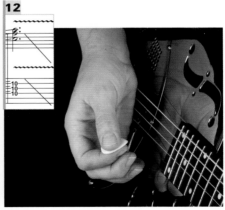

Bar 12 beat 3 *Allow the F chord to ring almost to the end of the third beat and then, without re-picking, move the slide down the neck to around the second fret. Then damp the strings with your palm as shown here.*

Bar 13 beat 1 *When you're playing slides on the top string only, angle the bottleneck away from the lower strings as is being shown here. This saves you from having to mute the lower strings.*

Bar 14 beat 4 *Slide pull-offs should be executed in exactly the same way as they would be with fingers, i.e. by flicking the slide slightly sideways as you release it from the strings.*

Bar 15 beat 2 *Use your pick, and your second (m) and third (a) fingers, to play the concluding chord slide in bar 15. This is more accurate than a strum and ensures all the notes are played simultaneously.*

Slide tails

When you see a straight, sloping line after a note or chord, it's indicating that you should slide down the strings before damping the note to provide a less abrupt cut-off. How far you slide is up to you; the further (and more slowly) you travel down the neck, the more dramatic the effect. Allow the note(s) to ring close to their full value and then, without re-picking, slide down the neck and damp the strings at the desired cut-off point.

CD

Lesson

27 Open D pentatonic scales

In this lesson you'll learn how to play the major pentatonic and major blues scales in open D tuning.

In this lesson you'll learn the final tuning of this book: open D. So, once you've worked through these last four lessons you will be comfortable playing in both open G and open D tunings. Some guitarists are happy to play in a variety of tunings, while others just stick to one. But by learning open G and open D tunings, one thing's for sure: you'll have kept your options open. Don't forget that by raising the pitch of open G tuning, it can be transposed to open A, and open D tuning can similarly be transposed to open E. The only difference is that you tune down for G or D tuning, and tune up for A or E tuning. Obviously, the range of notes that the

guitar can play changes, but all of the scale patterns and chord shapes remain the same. So, if you can play a G major pentatonic scale in open G tuning, then you can instantly play the A major pentatonic scale in open A. This is something that's well worth remembering when you're confronted with an awkward key or chord sequence that isn't working in your favorite tuning. So, effectively, by the time you've finished reading this book, you'll be able to play in five different tunings: E (standard tuning), and G, A, D, and E (open tunings).

Interval checker

By now you should be very familiar with the major pentatonic and major blues scales since you've already played them in the keys of G major (in standard E tuning) and C major (in open G tuning). Below are the note names in the new key of D major that we'll be focusing on in this lesson:

Major pentatonic

R   2   3   5   6   Oct

Major blues pentatonic

R   2   ♯2/♭3   3   5   6   Oct

The chords you'll need for this lesson:

 D

 D

EXERCISE 27.1

🎧 **Listen to track 50**

Many slide players prefer open D and (the related) open E tunings. That's because simply hitting all of the open strings will generate a root-position chord, making it ideal for playing open-position riffs. Before you start practicing the scales, practice alternating between the open D and fretted D shape on the twelfth fret. Once you've got the pitching, try adding slides before each chord (i.e. sliding up to the high D and down to the low D chord).

IMPORTANT TIP

Open D is a beautiful, resonant tuning. And, just as with open G tuning, when you lay your slide across the strings you instantly get a major chord. The advantage of open D tuning is that the note on the sixth string is the root note of the chord. This makes a big difference when you're playing riffs, especially in open position. So, take some time out to familiarize yourself with the sound of this great tuning by alternating between the open and twelfth fret shapes as illustrated in Exercise 27.1.

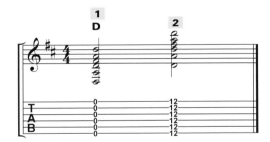

Start your strum from the sixth string, sweeping your pick evenly across all of the strings.

When playing the high D chord, you need to ensure that your slide is directly above the twelfth fret, not behind it.

EXERCISE 27.2

🎧 **Listen to track 51**
This is the open D major pentatonic scale with its root note on the open sixth string. Notice how all of the chord tones of the D major triad (R-3-5) are present in the open strings. Visualize the open chord as you play the scale notes; this will help you to distinguish between chord tones and non-chord tones—extremely useful knowledge when you're improvising. As always, the scale should be practiced both ascending and descending.

When you're playing the low notes on the sixth string, mute the higher strings by resting your (m) and (a) fingers on them as shown here.

Make sure that your slide is clear of the strings before picking the open fifth string on beat four as shown here.

Use down-picks throughout to create nice, clear notes. This photograph shows the pick striking the second string with a down-pick on beat one of the final bar.

EXERCISE 27.3

🎧 **Listen to track 52**

This example adds the "blue" note (E♯) to generate the major pentatonic blues scale. Just as you found when adding the blue note to the G major pentatonic, this involves moving the slide in smaller increments (half steps) than before. Don't forget to keep checking that your slide is directly above the fret and not behind it.

When playing the low notes on the sixth string, angle the slide into the notes so that it's raised off the higher strings. This will prevent you from having to mute all the strings between the notes.

To generate clean notes without an audible slide between them, always damp the last note before picking the next by touching the string with the side of your thumb.

Get into the habit of resting your picking fingers on the strings, even when you're not using the slide. This photograph shows the fingers (m) and (a) resting on the first and second strings as the open third string is picked.

CD

Lesson

tracks 53, 54, 55

28 Open D slide licks

Three exciting slide licks that illustrate the versatility of
open D tuning.

In this lesson you'll learn three cool licks with a distinctly bluegrass flavor. Once you've mastered them you'll start to see why many slide players favor open D tuning. Although open G is a great tuning, open D just seems more suited to slide playing. There are two reasons for this: 1) barring across any fret with the slide produces a full major chord with its root note on the sixth string and 2) located within easy reach of this chord shape are all of the essential notes you'll need for playing hot country slide. As we discovered in the earlier lessons, slide guitarists don't really think the

same way as regular guitar players; once you're wearing that bottleneck you're quite limited as far as chord shapes go. So it just makes more sense to orientate your ideas either along an individual string, or across the strings using the six-string major chord as the "home" shape. Once you start to get the hang of string muting and accurate pitching, you'll find that playing slide is very intuitive in open D. And don't forget that slide playing isn't about playing a lot of notes; it's about dialing up those wonderfully primeval sounds that can send shivers up your audience's spine.

Open D note pool

The notes of the major and minor pentatonic scales are all within easy reach in open D tuning. The example below illustrates how these two scales provide an open D "note pool"; perfect for playing country licks. The notes on the twelfth fret are D major chord tones; the lower notes are D minor pentatonic scale notes (apart from the major second), and the higher notes are D major pentatonic scale notes.

* The major 2nd falls above the slide on the 4th string and below the slide on the 3rd string.

The chords you'll need for this lesson:

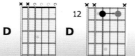

EXERCISE 28.1

🎧 **Listen to track 53**

By sliding a half step above the major pentatonic scale notes on the second, fourth, and fifth strings you can easily add the minor seventh and minor third "blue notes" to the scale. This is a great way to create bluegrass-flavored riffs, just as in this exercise.

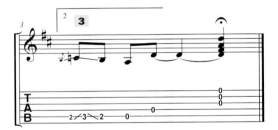

As you pick the first note in the pickup bar, your slide should already be in position above the second fret. Notice how only the tip of the slide will be used to fret the note in order to avoid unnecessary string damping.

This photograph illustrates the (m) and (a) fingers correctly resting on the higher strings while the slide on the fifth string is picked at the beginning of bar 2.

By angling your slide so that it just lifts off of the higher strings, and using only the tip of the slide to play the note, you will be able to produce a much "cleaner" sound when playing on the lower strings.

EXERCISE 28.2

Listen to track 54

This lick illustrates how effective the horizontal approach (i.e. playing along a single string) can be in open D tuning, particularly when allowing low, open strings to ring throughout the phrase as they do here. When played on a resonator guitar, this lick has an unmistakeably bluegrass flavor.

When fretting the notes on the second string, make sure your slide is positioned so that only the tip is used to play the notes as shown here. This will allow the open strings to ring throughout.

When playing the slide up to the F on beat three of bar 1, make sure that your slide stops directly above the eighth fret as shown in this photograph. Since this is a "blue" note it can be played slightly sharp if desired by positioning the slide just in front of the fret.

As you pick the low F in the final bar, your (m) and (a) fingers should also be resting on the second and third strings as shown here. This effectively stops the previous note from ringing on and also mutes the adjacent third string.

EXERCISE 28.3

🎧 **Listen to track 55**

Based around the twelfth fret D chord shape, this lick adds notes from the "note pool" (see page 132) to the regular major pentatonic notes. This allows non-pentatonic notes such as the F and C natural to be incorporated into the lick. Because this lick traverses four strings, it's great for practicing and perfecting your string-muting technique.

IMPORTANT TIP

Just sliding into a chord note from two frets below or two frets above (see the "note pool" on page 132 for available notes) sounds cool when you're playing with a bottleneck. Practice this on all of the strings until you can accurately slide into all of the notes on the twelfth fret; this will help you to develop a consistent and accurate technique.

As you move your pick onto the fourth string to play the third note (D), allow the side of your thumb to make contact with the fifth string. This will mute the previous note, effectively preventing the two notes from sounding together.

The second note (F natural) on the third beat should be played with an up-pick as shown. Notice how the (m) and (a) fingers are resting on the first and second strings, muting the high B and preventing it from ringing into the next note.

Don't lay the slide across all six strings when you're playing notes on the higher strings. Here you can see just the tip of the slide is used to play the second string notes at the beginning of the second bar.

CD

Lesson

29 Open D fingerstyle riffs

Combining fingerstyle and slide techniques creates a potent combo hotter than steak and pepper sauce!

Open tuning is perfect for fingerstyle guitar; you can play cool picking patterns without even having to fret a chord shape. And just a few picked open strings is sometimes all you need as the starting-point for a great riff. Once you've created a simple picking pattern, stick the bottleneck on your third finger and start adding in a few slides; it really is that easy. We'll be using this simple approach to create three smokin' slide riffs that steadily ramp up picking-hand intensity, building your skills progressively. As we've already learned in earlier lessons, by wearing the slide on your third finger, your first and second fingers remain free to damp the strings behind the slide. When you're playing riffs in first position (i.e. based on the open D shape), you can use these fingers to add fretted notes or chord shapes between slides. This technique is used by electric and acoustic players alike, but lends itself particularly well to fingerstyle acoustic slide-playing. You can play melodies on the top strings while adding bass notes on the lower, or add a mix of fretted and slide melody notes to an alternating bass pattern played on the low strings. One thing's for sure: you'll be taking your accompanying skills to the next level in this lesson.

IMPORTANT TIP

Always learn the two parts of a fingerstyle arrangement separately. Remember that notes with the stems up are played with the fingers (*i*, *m*, and *a*) and notes with the stems down should be played with the thumb (*p*). Once you can play the parts independently, start adding the melody (stems up) to the bassline (stems down) one note at a time, identifying whether the note should be pinched with the bass (played simultaneously) or between bass notes (syncopated).

The chords you'll need for this lesson:

Open D chord shapes

As you'll discover in Exercise 29.3, exciting patterns can be created when slide notes and fretted notes are mixed. You already know that sounding the open strings produces a D major chord, but fret one or two notes with your first and second fingers and you can change the sound of this chord dramatically. You'll find it's easy to create your own cool fingerstyle slide riffs using the useful shapes below.

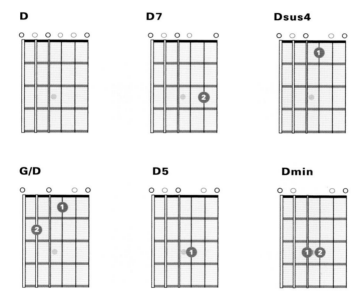

EXERCISE 29.1

🎧 **Listen to track 56**

This exercise illustrates that by adding a few bass notes to a succession of slide chords, you can create an exiting, full-sounding riff. All of the chords are played on the off-beats between the bass notes to create a syncopated rhythm. This makes the riff a little more difficult to play, but a lot more interesting to listen to.

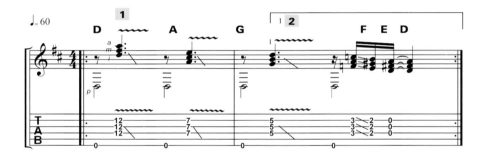

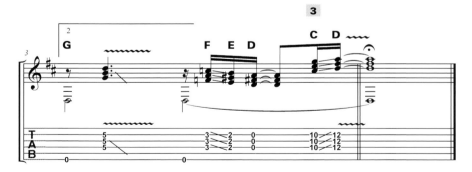

It's important to keep your slide high on the strings so that it doesn't damp the open sixth string; this note must be allowed to ring throughout. Notice how the first and second fingers should trail behind the slide, resting across the strings and preventing any unwanted resonance.

Pick the bass notes with your thumb (p) and use your fingers (i, m, and a) to pick the three-note chord. Your picking hand should remain still, hovering above the strings once you've played the chord as shown here.

The final chord should be played on the ninth fret (B major) and slid up to the twelfth fret without picking. Keep your slide parallel with the frets as you slide to keep the notes in tune.

EXERCISE 29.2

🎧 **Listen to track 57**

In this exercise a linear melodic phrase is supported by a constant *alternating thumb* bassline. Alternating basslines are a little tricky to get together at first but well worth persevering with. It's a great technique for creating exciting fingerstyle accompaniments.

It's important keep your slide very high on the strings when playing the melody notes to keep it clear of the open fourth string. This photograph shows the F♯ on beat one of the first bar played with the slide only covering the first and second strings.

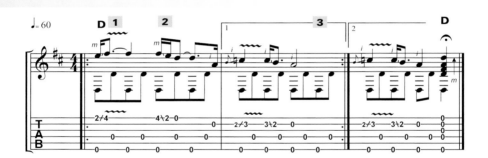

To keep the lower string muted, rest your first finger (i) on the second string while picking the melody on the first string with your second (m) finger, as shown here.

Keep your thumb constantly alternating between the sixth and fourth strings. This photograph shows the thumb returning to play the sixth string after picking the fourth string on the third beat of bar 2.

EXERCISE 29.3

🎧 **Listen to track 58**

In this last exercise only the notes on the first string are played with the slide. The lower melody notes are fretted notes played with the first and second fingers. The melody is heavily syncopated, so it's important to start your practice much slower than the indicated tempo of 80 bpm.

The first melody note (F) is played as a pinch with the bass note on the second half of beat one. Here you can see the thumb striking the fourth string while the second finger (m) picks the first string.

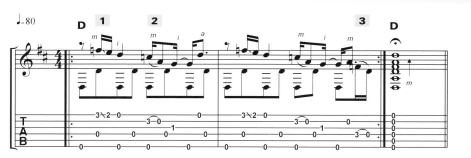

On the third beat of bar 1 the melody note (C) should be fretted, not played with the slide. Release the finger with a sideways motion as illustrated to play the pull-off to the lower note.

At the end of the second bar the last bass note is played as a pull-off to the open fourth string (F to D). Use your second finger to fret the F, pulling-off to the open string with a sideways flicking motion in order to generate a strong resolution note.

CD

Lesson

"Goin' Home to Kentucky"

Find out how the pros deal with the problem of playing in minor keys when you learn this bluegrass-style tune.

Since all of the open D tuned slide examples have so far been in the key of D major, you could be forgiven for thinking that this tuning is limited to one key. You may have also wondered, since the guitar is tuned to a major chord, how it is possible to play over minor chords. So, in this lesson you'll be learning how to play in the keys of A minor and C major. This illustrates the versatility of open D tuning perfectly. The verse section of this tune is in A minor, while the chorus modulates to C major (the relative major key). A quick glance at the time signature and you'll notice that this tune is also in 2/2 or "cut time." Remember

that cut time contains exactly the same number of notes as 4/4, i.e. one whole note in every bar. However, the pulse is in cut time and is counted in half notes, not quarter notes. Listen to the bass on the CD and you'll notice that the bassline plays only half notes. This is typical of the country "cut-time" groove. For an in-depth explanation of cut time, have another look at Lesson 15. Don't worry if you've forgotten this because we've covered a lot of ground since that lesson. After all, learning is about repetition and reinforcements, that's why musicians spend so much of their time practicing!

Double-stop slides

Double-stop slides feature throughout this tune, so it's well worth taking time out to make sure you're playing them right. Sometimes the slide into a note, double stop, or chord can be freely interpreted. However, when a slide has been notated with a precise starting-point and a specific rhythm, it's important to play it as written. The example above focuses on the two chromatic slides that are used before the F and G chords in this piece. Keep your slide parallel with the frets and play the rhythm as indicated, just as you would when playing fretted notes.

The chord you'll need for this lesson: F

Be a better player

Warm up by practicing the major and relative minor scales

So far we've avoided full major and minor scales because we haven't needed to use them. However, it would be a good idea to practice the scales below before you start learning this tune as they're both featured in the melody. Don't forget that you should always practice scales ascending and descending, ensuring that you're damping behind and in front of the slide, and that your slide is directly over the fret.

A natural minor scale (open D tuning)

C major scale (open D tuning)

"Goin' Home to Kentucky"
Listen to track 59, play with track 60

When you listen to the melody on the CD you'll notice that it seems to "float" over the accompaniment. That's one of the great facets of slide guitar; by using slides and slurs before a note it's very easy to create the illusion of a laid-back performance. However, in reality, the melody is rhythmically accurate, with all of the notes falling exactly where they should. So before you get too bogged down in the mechanics of playing the notes, make sure you know exactly where they should be played, rhythmically speaking. Many of the phrases in this piece actually begin on the off-beat of the preceding bar (just like the first note). This helps to create the free-and-easy feel of the melody. However, if you don't start your phrases exactly in the right place, they really will be free and easy, but not in a good way! Achieving a critical balance between good timekeeping and a relaxed groove is something that all musicians continually strive for; it can only be achieved with daily practice.

"Goin' Home to Kentucky"

Verse

Chorus

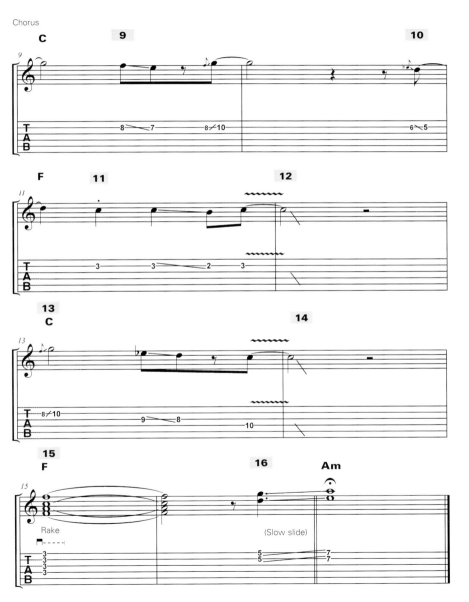

Continue for step by steps ▶▶

Bar 1 beat 2 *To play the staccato D note on the second beat, touch the string with your second finger (m) as soon as you've played the note. Notice how the pick simultaneously moves over the third string ready to play the next note.*

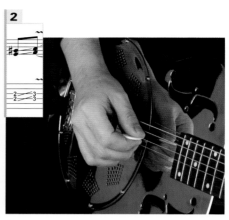

Bar 2 beat 4 *You can play the chromatic double stop using hybrid picking (as is being illustrated here) or a single down-pick. The combination of pick and fingers produces a pedal-steel-like sound.*

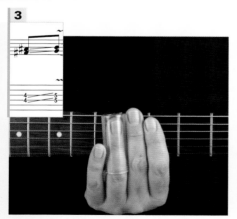

Bar 3 beat 4 *It's important to keep your slide parallel to the frets when playing double-stop slides. Even a slight deviation from this position will result in out-of-tune notes.*

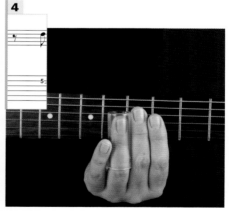

Bar 4 beat 4 *The slide into the second statement of the melody should begin with your bottleneck directly above the fifth fret, as illustrated. Remember that this note should be played on the off-beat of beat four.*

Bar 5 beat 2 *Mute the ringing second string before you play the A on the second beat. This is achieved by touching the string with the side of your thumb as you move your pick into position to play the note.*

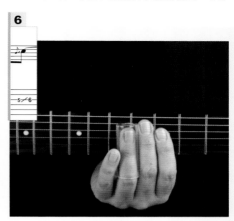

Bar 5 beat 4 *The grace-note slide at the end of this bar slides into the C which is the minor third of the chord. Make sure that your slide travels no further than the sixth fret or you will produce a very dissonant note.*

Bar 7 beat 4 *To keep the first and second strings muted when playing the double-stop slide on the fourth beat, rest your remaining picking-hand fingers on the strings as is shown here.*

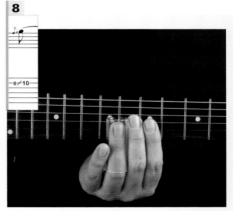

Bar 8 beat 4 *To avoid having to damp all of the strings all of the time, keep your slide focused on just the top three strings when playing melody notes on the second string as is illustrated here.*

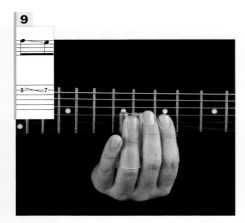

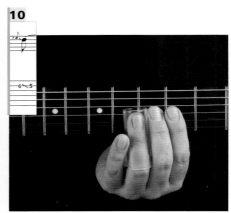

Bar 9 beat 3 *The slide from F to E on the third beat of bar 9 moves a half step (one fret) only. Before you pick the string, the slide should be positioned directly above the eighth fret as seen here.*

Bar 10 beat 4 *The grace-note slide at the end of bar 10 should be played quickly and accurately. Be careful not to "overshoot" the target fret or you will produce a flat pitch. Your slide should come to rest directly above the fifth fret as shown.*

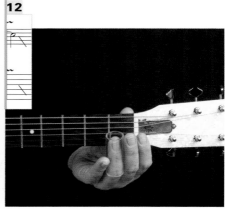

Bar 11 beat 2 *Don't forget that a staccato note must be muted as soon as it is played. Here the C on the second beat has been muted by quickly touching it with the tip of the first finger, just before the note is re-picked.*

Bar 12 beat 1 *Remember that the downward line after a note indicates a slide trail-off. Release the note by dragging the slide down the string (without re-picking), lifting it off the strings on the first fret as shown here.*

13

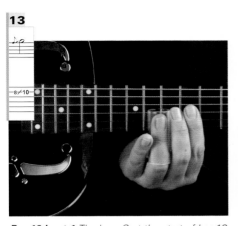

Bar 13 beat 1 *The long G at the start of bar 13 should be allowed to ring without adding any vibrato. It's important to ensure that a long note is perfectly in tune by checking the slide is directly above the fret as shown here.*

14

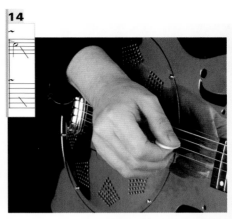

Bar 14 beat 1 *The sustained C note should be played with vibrato in this bar. However, vibrato can generate unwanted string noise, so mute the top three strings by resting your remaining fingers on them as shown here.*

15

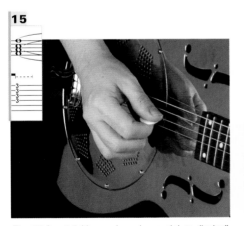

Bar 15 beat 1 *Use a slow down-pick to "rake" across the strings when playing the F chord. This photograph shows the pick in position on the fourth string just before the chord is played.*

16

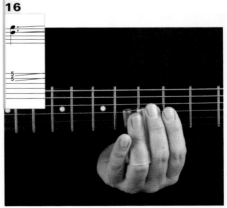

Bar 16 beat 3 *The double-stop slide on the top strings should be played slowly, moving your slide up the neck at a constant speed while keeping it parallel to the frets. Start with your slide directly above the fifth fret as shown.*

CHORD LIBRARY

Notation guide

Open position (first fret) chord box:

Chord box beginning on fifth fret:

✖   open string *not* played

○   open string (root note) played

○   open string (chord note) played

●   root note

●   chord note

●━● barre or semi-barre

Note: circled numbers indicate correct fretting-hand fingering.

CHAPTER 2

In this section you'll be able to find the shapes for many useful sixth, seventh, ninth, and diminished chords. These chords will not only expand your chord vocabulary, but will also work well as a substitute for more basic voicings, adding a professional touch to your songs and accompaniments. Each chord has been categorized by its root note so that you can find the chord you want, quickly and easily. You can also use this resource to experiment with different chord types. So, for example, if your chord chart suggests a simple C chord you could try playing C6, Cmaj7, or even C7 instead; you'll find them all on the same page. If you're a songwriter, this section of the book could prove to be an invaluable resource, inspiring your chord choices and helping you to create exciting new progressions.

To provide you with the most practical and useful chords, the lowest available shape on the guitar neck is always given. In addition, each chord has the relevant CAGED shape indicated beneath its name (see Lesson 17, pages 77–81 for more on CAGED shapes). In this way you'll ultimately be able to learn the five shapes for every chord as you work through the library.

C root

C6 (CM6)
SHAPE 3

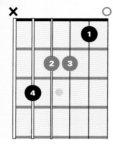

Cmaj7 (CΔ, CM7)
SHAPE 3

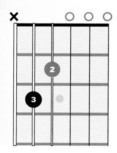

Cmin7 (Cm7, C-7)
SHAPE 4

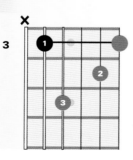

C root

C7 (Cdom7)
SHAPE 3

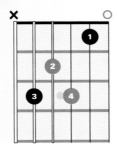

C9 (Cdom9)
SHAPE 3

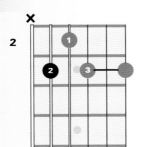

C°7 (Cdim7)
SHAPE 4

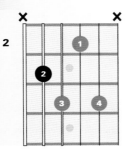

C♯ root

C♯6 (C♯M6)
SHAPE 3

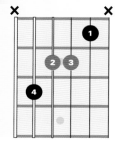

C♯maj7 (C♯△, C♯M7)
SHAPE 3

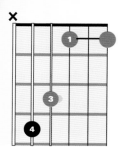

C♯min7 (C♯m7, C♯-7)
SHAPE 4

C♯ root

C♯7 (C♯dom7)
SHAPE 3

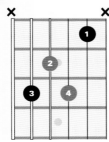

C♯9 (C♯dom9)
SHAPE 3

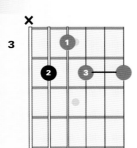

C♯°7 (C♯dim7)
SHAPE 4

D root

D6 (DM6)
SHAPE 2

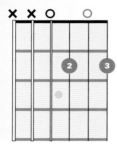

Dmaj7 (DΔ, DM7)
SHAPE 2

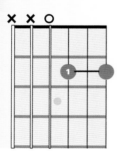

Dmin7 (Dm7, D-7)
SHAPE 2

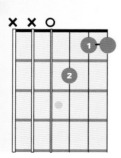

D root

D7 (Ddom7)
SHAPE 2

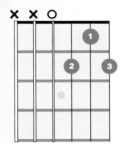

D9 (Ddom9)
SHAPE 3

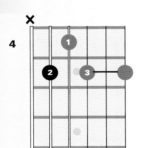

D°7 (Ddim7)
SHAPE 2

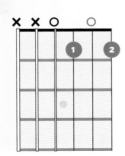

E♭ root

E♭6 (E♭M6)

SHAPE 2

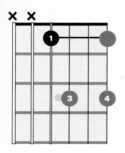

E♭maj7 (E♭△, E♭M7)

SHAPE 2

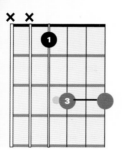

E♭min7 (E♭m7, E♭-7)

SHAPE 2

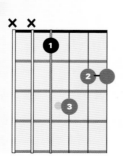

E♭ root

E♭7 (E♭dom7)
SHAPE 2

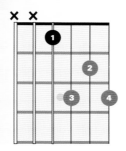

E♭9 (E♭dom9)
SHAPE 3

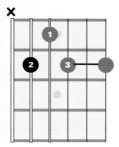

E♭°7 (E♭dim7)
SHAPE 2

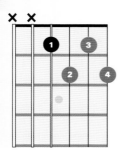

E root

E6 (EM6)
SHAPE 1

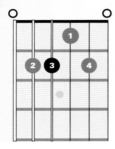

Emaj7 (E△, EM7)
SHAPE 2

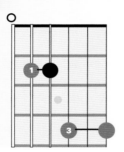

Emin7 (Em7, E-7)
SHAPE 1

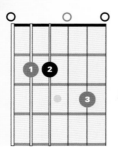

E root

E7 (Edom7)
SHAPE 1

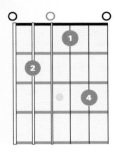

E9 (Edom9)
(open 6th string optional)
SHAPE 1

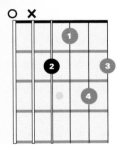

E°7 (Edim7)
(open 6th string optional)
SHAPE 2

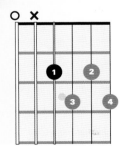

F root

F6 (FM6)
SHAPE 1

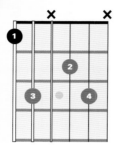

Fmaj7 (FΔ, FM7)
SHAPE 1

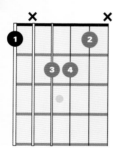

Fmin7 (Fm7, F-7)
SHAPE 1

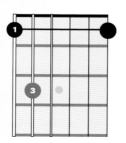

F root

F7 (Fdom7)
SHAPE 1

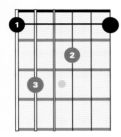

F9 (Fdom9)
SHAPE 1

F°7 (Fdim7)
SHAPE 2

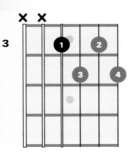

F♯ root

F♯6 (F♯M6)
SHAPE 1

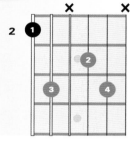

F♯maj7 (F♯△, F♯M7)
SHAPE 1

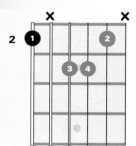

F♯min7 (F♯m7, F♯-7)
SHAPE 1

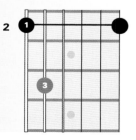

F♯ root

F♯7 (F♯dom7)

SHAPE 1

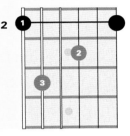

F♯9 (F♯dom9)

SHAPE 1

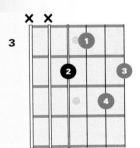

F♯°7 (F♯dim7)

SHAPE 1

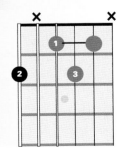

G root

G6 (GM6)
SHAPE 5

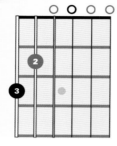

Gmaj7 (GΔ, GM7)
SHAPE 5

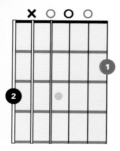

Gmin7 (Gm7, G-7)
SHAPE 1

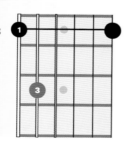

G root

G7 (Gdom7)

SHAPE 5

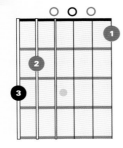

G9 (Gdom9)

SHAPE 5

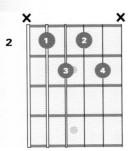

G°7 (Gdim7)

SHAPE 1

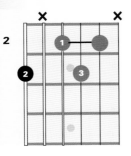

A♭ root

A♭6 (A♭M6)
SHAPE 1

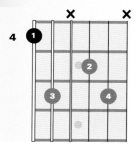

A♭maj7 (A♭△, A♭M7)
SHAPE 1

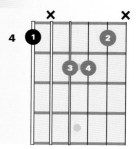

A♭min7 (A♭m7, A♭-7)
SHAPE 1

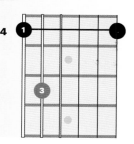

A♭ root

A♭7 (A♭dom7)
SHAPE 1

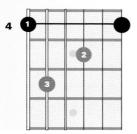

A♭9 (A♭dom9)
SHAPE 5

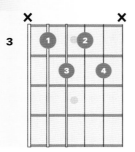

A♭°7 (A♭dim7)
SHAPE 1

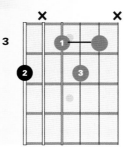

A root

A6 (AM6)
SHAPE 4

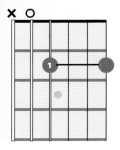

Amaj7 (AΔ, AM7)
SHAPE 4

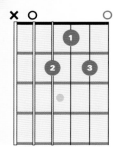

Amin7 (Am7, A-7)
SHAPE 4

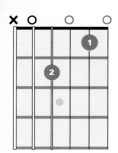

A root

A7 (Adom7)
SHAPE 4

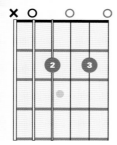

A9 (Adom9)
SHAPE 5

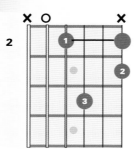

A°7 (Adim7)
SHAPE 4

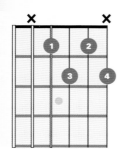

B♭ root

B♭6 (B♭M6)

SHAPE 4

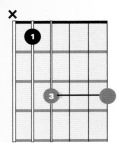

B♭maj7 (B♭△, B♭M7)

SHAPE 4

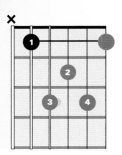

B♭min7 (B♭m7, B♭-7)

SHAPE 4

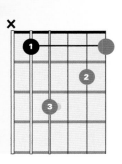

B♭ root

B♭7 (B♭dom7)
SHAPE 4

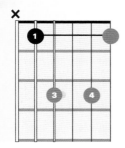

B♭9 (B♭dom9)
SHAPE 3

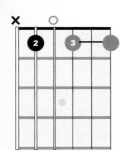

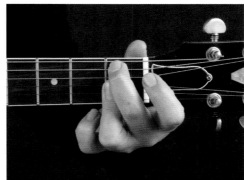

B♭°7 (B♭dim7)
SHAPE 4

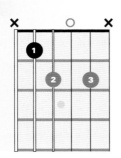

B root

B6 (BM6)
SHAPE 4

Bmaj7 (B△, BM7)
SHAPE 4

Bmin7 (Bm7, B-7)
SHAPE 3

B root

B7 (Bdom7)
SHAPE 3

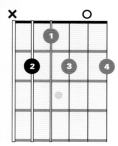

B9 (Bdom9)
SHAPE 3

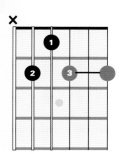

B°7 (Bdim7)
SHAPE 4

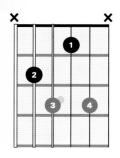

PENTATONIC SCALE LIBRARY

Notation guide

Open position (first fret) scale box:

Scale box starting at the seventh fret:

✖ open string *not* played

O open string (root note) played

O open string (chord note) played

● root note

● scale note

● "blue" note

Note: circled numbers indicate correct fretting-hand fingering.

7

CHAPTER 3

This resource will enable you to find any major or minor pentatonic scale you need, quickly and easily. The scales have been organized so that the lowest CAGED shape is always given first; the remaining shapes then ascend the fretboard in order, building a complete five-pattern sequence that maps the entire guitar neck. Notes are color-coded using the same principle as in the chord library, making it easy to quickly locate those all-important root notes. The "blue notes" (see page 41) have also been included in both the major and minor pentatonic scales; these are colored blue (what else!) so you can instantly identify them. Each pattern has been constructed with logical fingering, making it easy to include or omit the blue notes when you're practicing. Practicing the scales with and without these notes will improve your ear, your technique, and ultimately your improvising skills. You'll find that this section of the book will become a useful resource, invaluable for creating cool licks, solos, riffs, and chord embellishments.

PRACTICE TIPS

• Learn all five shapes in sequence for all keys.

• Learn the open strings available in any key. These notes are essential for creating authentic-sounding country licks, whether you're playing bluegrass or contemporary country rock.

• Learn the corresponding CAGED chord shape for every scale shape. This will ultimately lead to total fretboard fluency; so with practice you will be able to play licks anywhere on the neck, in any key.

C major pentatonic

| R | 2 | ♯2/♭3 | 3 | 5 | 6 | OCT |

SHAPE 3

SHAPE 4

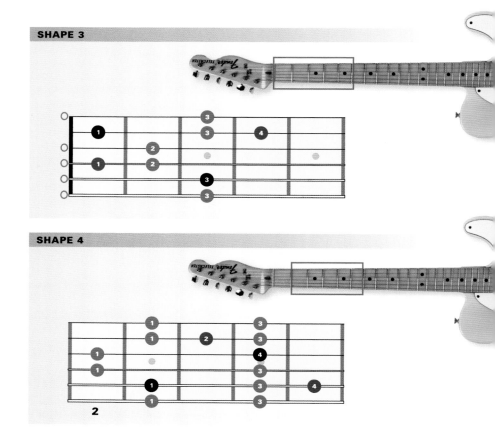

SHAPE 5

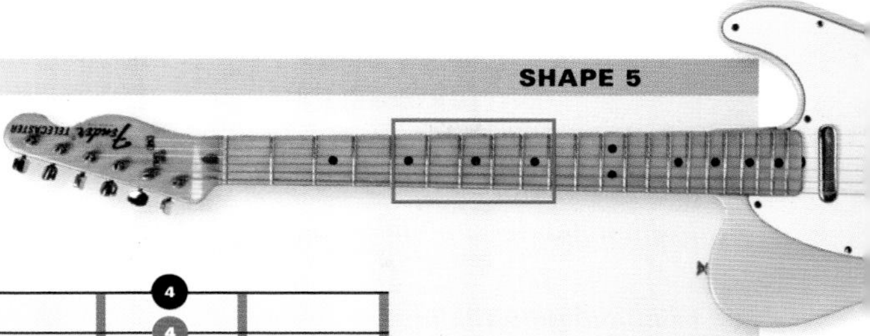

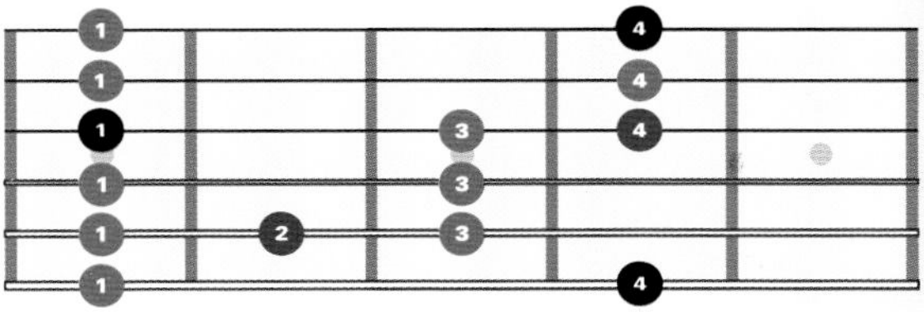

5

SHAPE 1

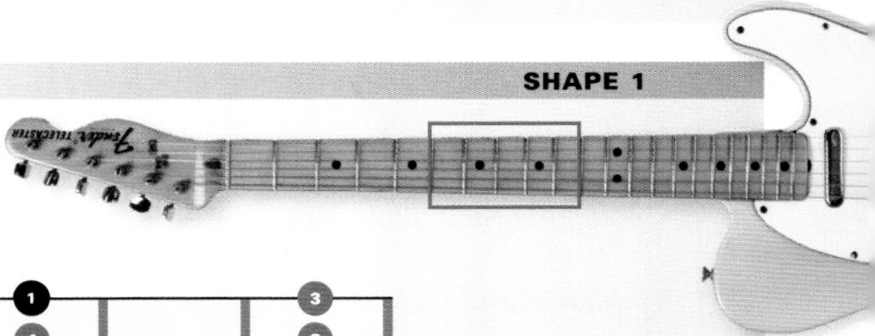

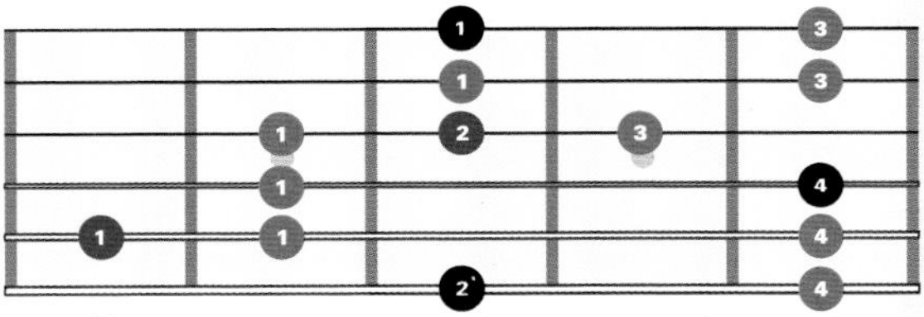

6

SHAPE 2

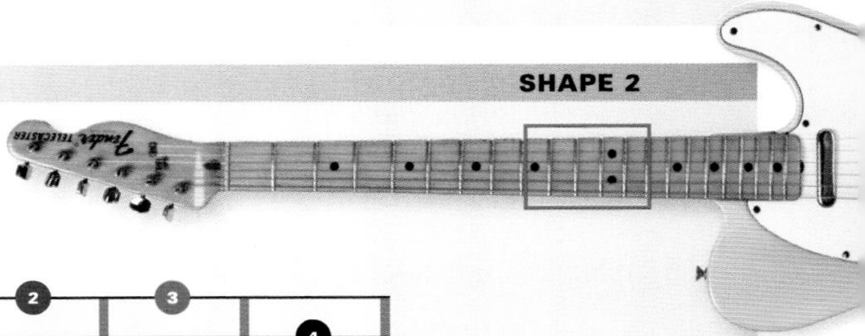

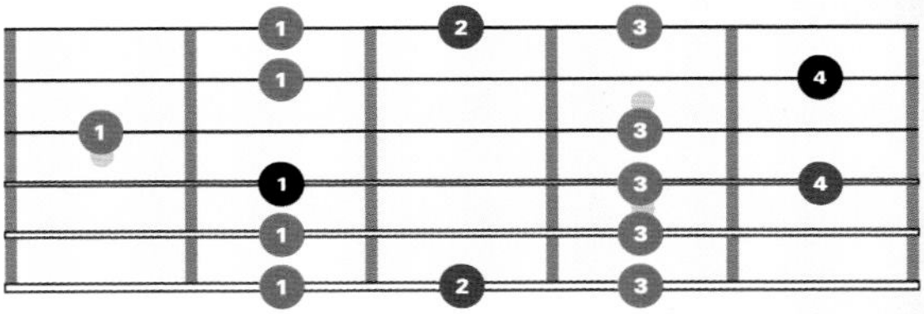

9

C# major pentatonic

| R | 2 | #2/♭3 | 3 | 5 | 6 | OCT |

SHAPE 3

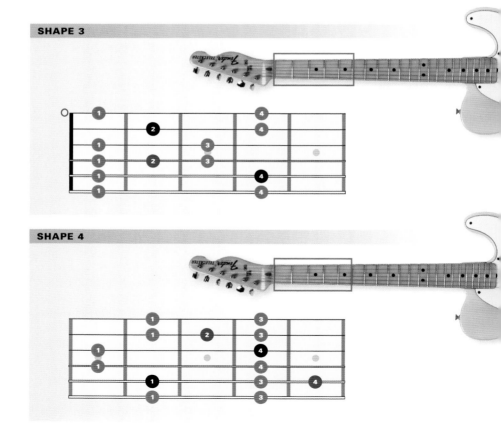

SHAPE 4

SHAPE 5

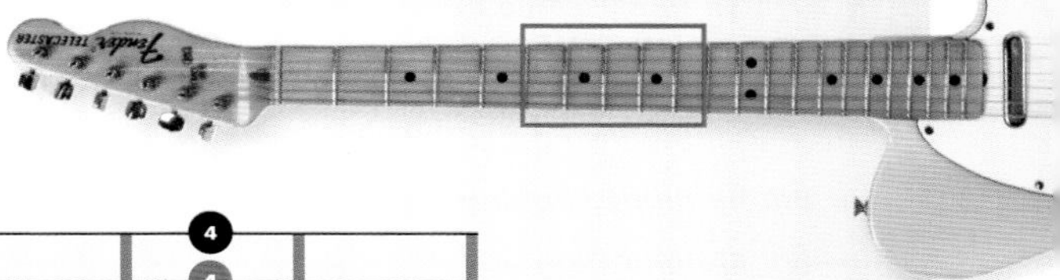

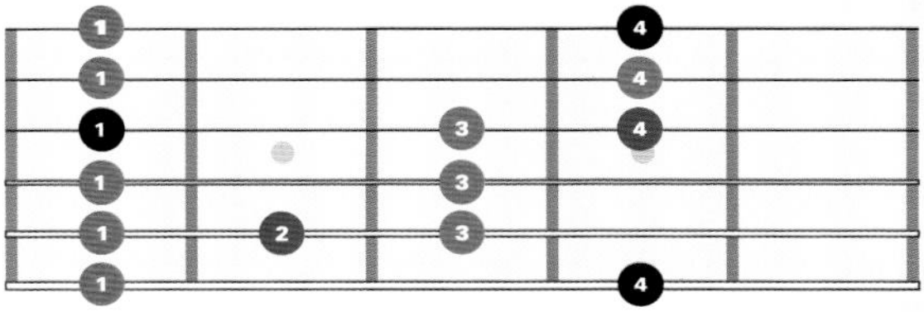

6

SHAPE 1

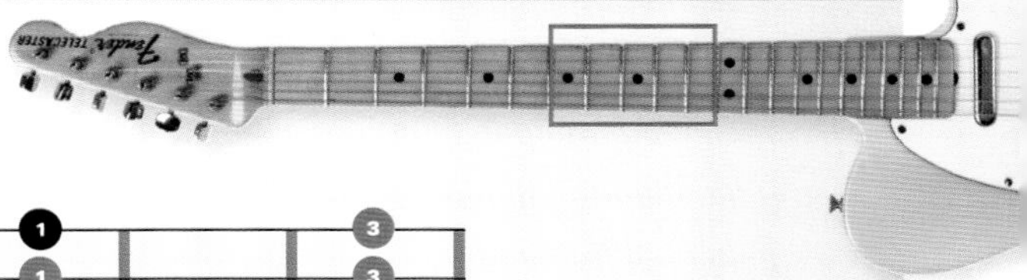

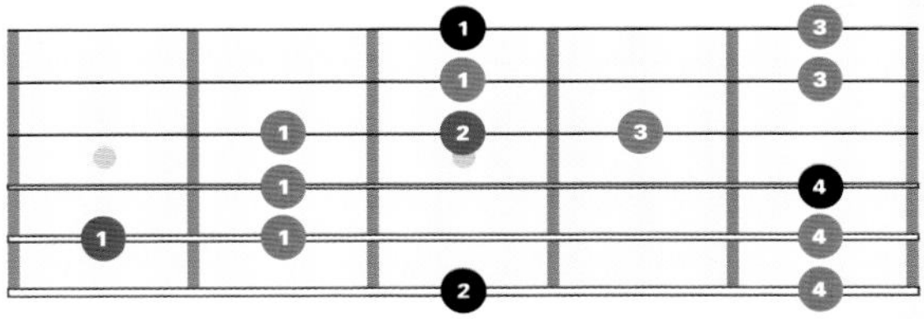

7

SHAPE 2

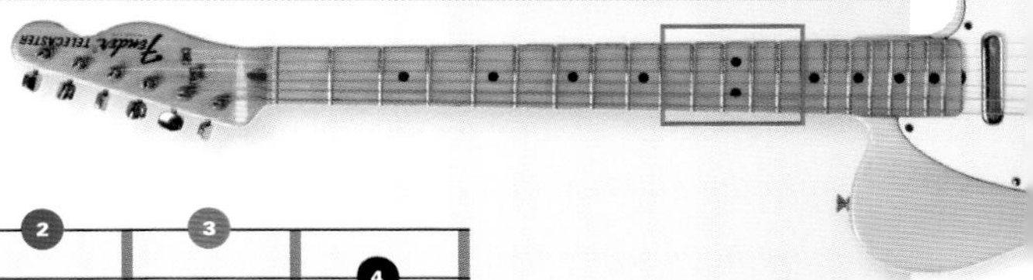

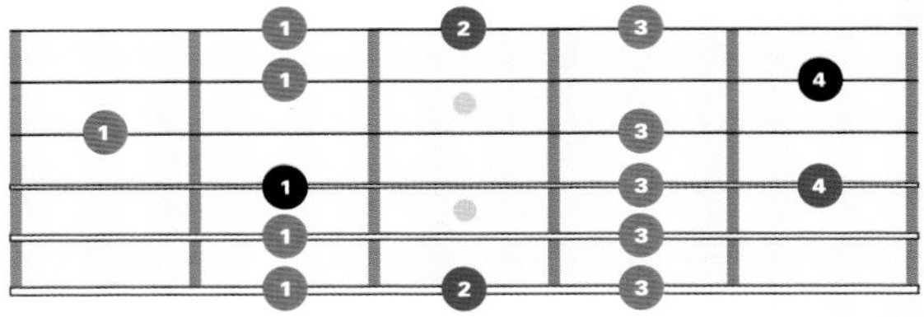

10

D major pentatonic

R	2	#2/b3	3	5	6	OCT

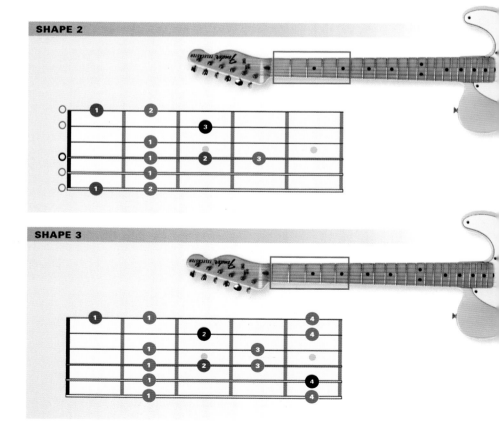

SHAPE 2

SHAPE 3

SHAPE 4

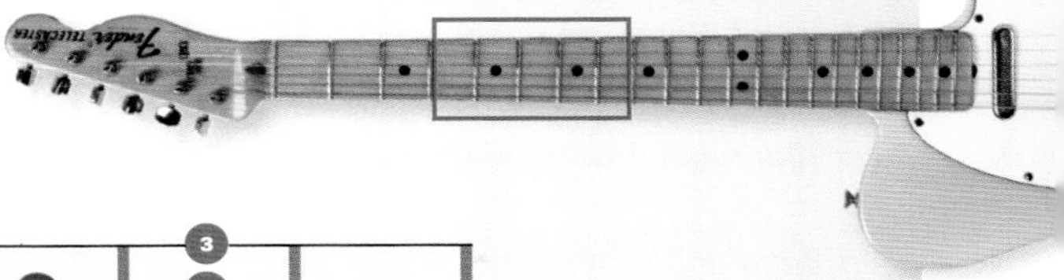

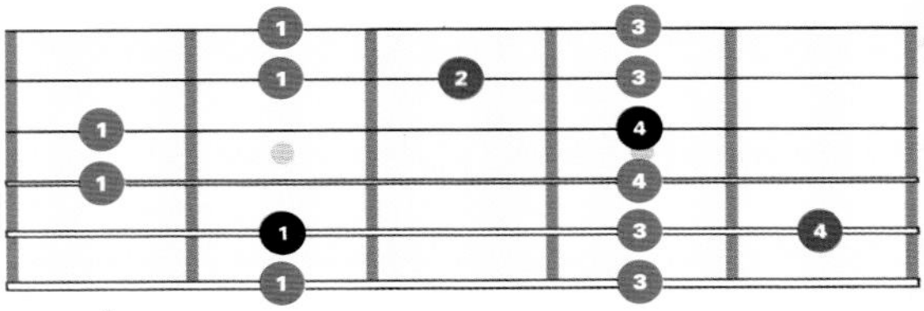

4

SHAPE 5

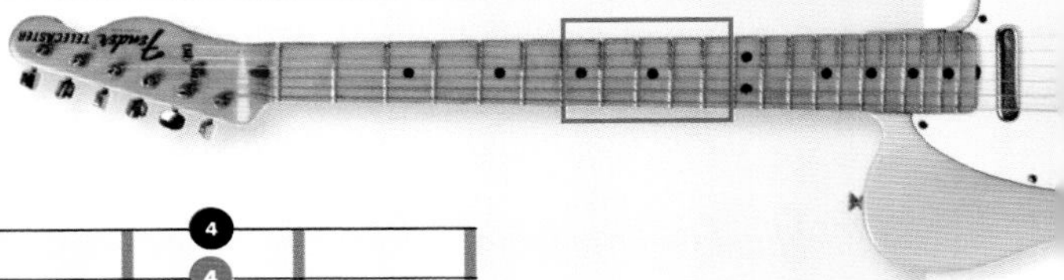

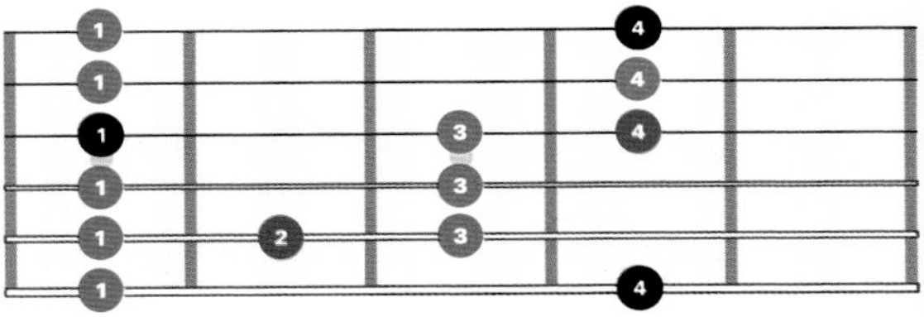

7

SHAPE 1

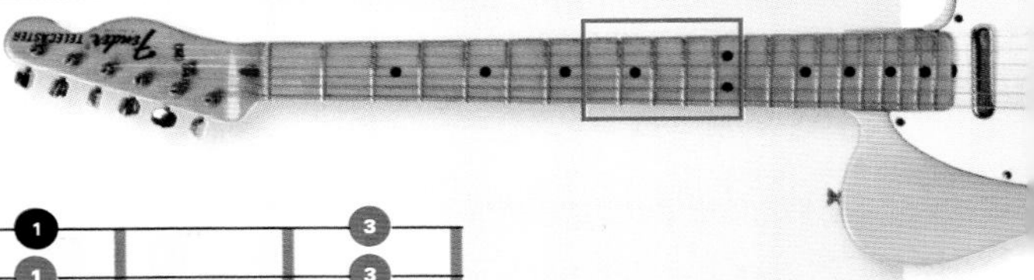

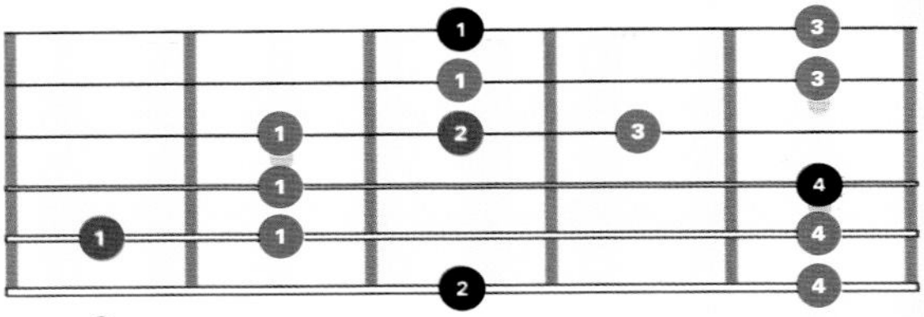

8

E♭ major pentatonic

| R | 2 | #2/♭3 | 3 | 5 | 6 | OCT |

SHAPE 2

SHAPE 3

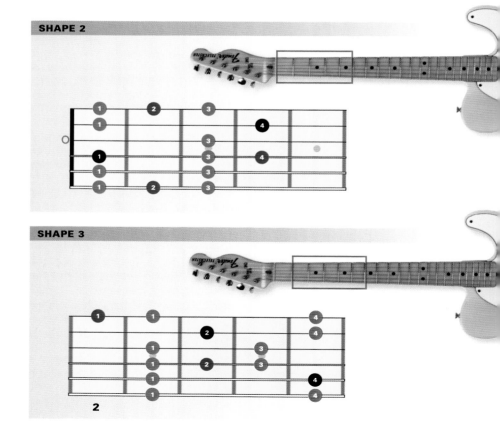

SHAPE 4

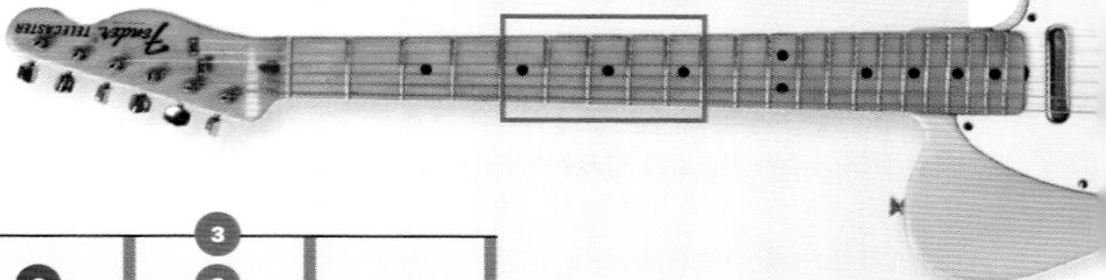

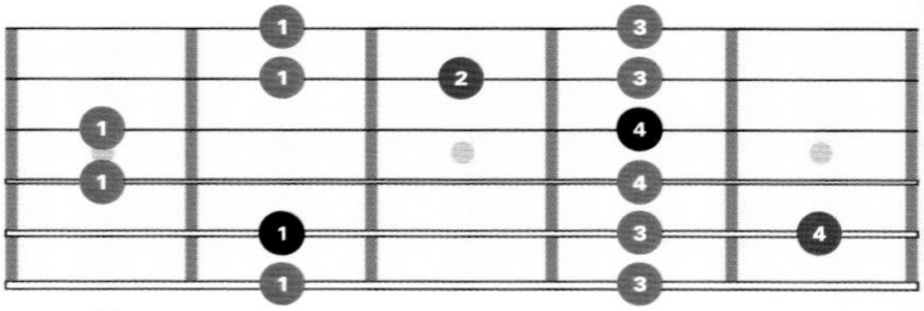

5

SHAPE 5

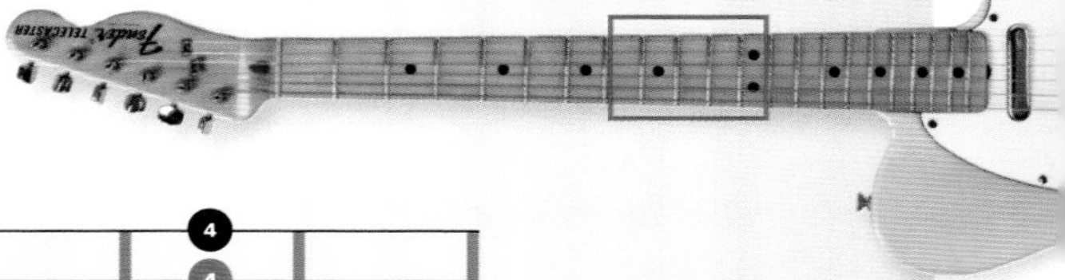

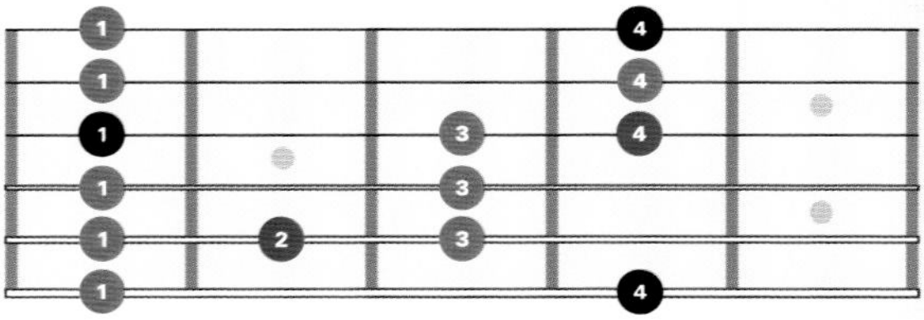

8

SHAPE 1

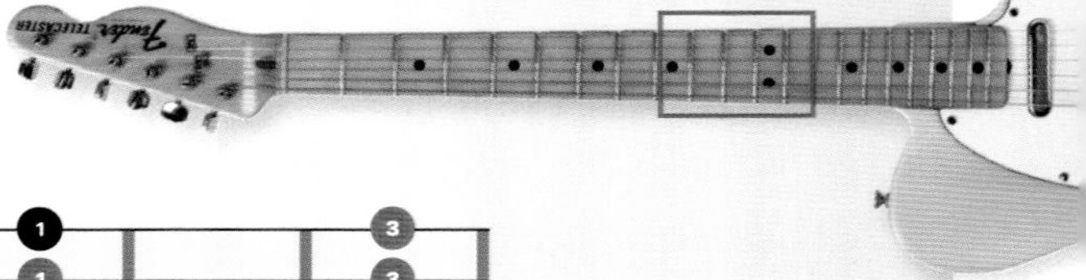

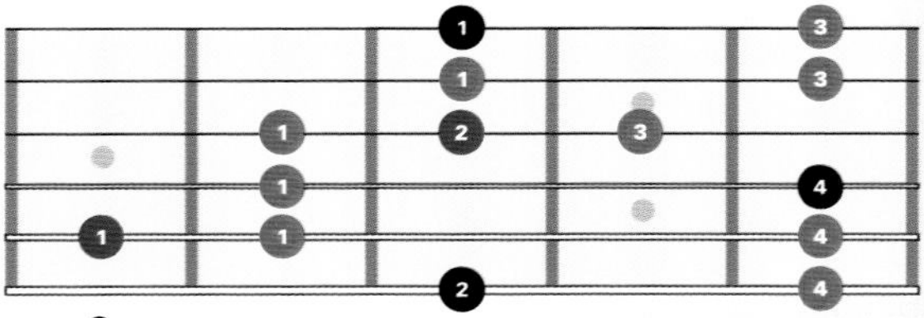

9

E major pentatonic

| R | 2 | #2/b3 | 3 | 5 | 6 | OCT |

SHAPE 1

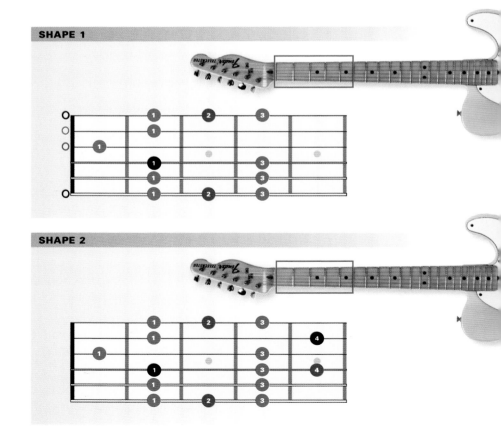

SHAPE 2

SHAPE 3

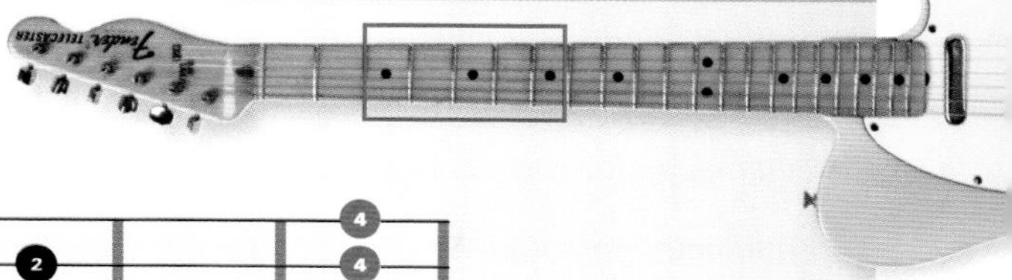

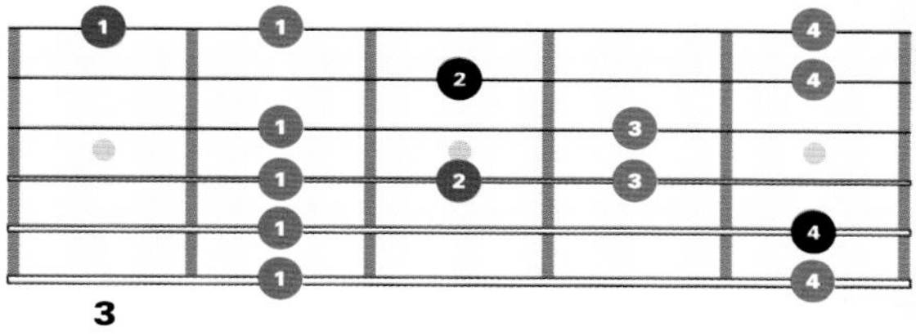

3

SHAPE 4

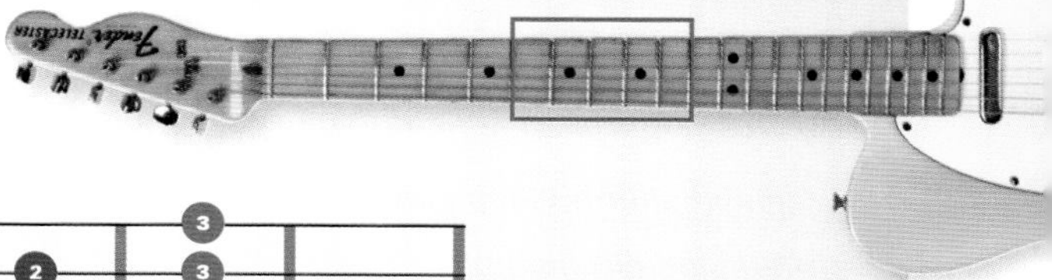

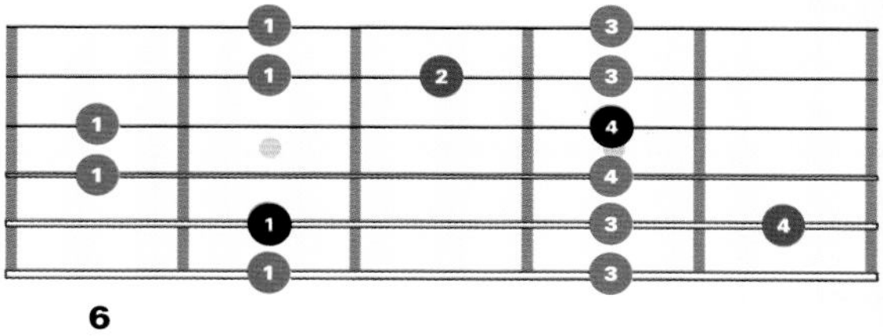

6

SHAPE 5

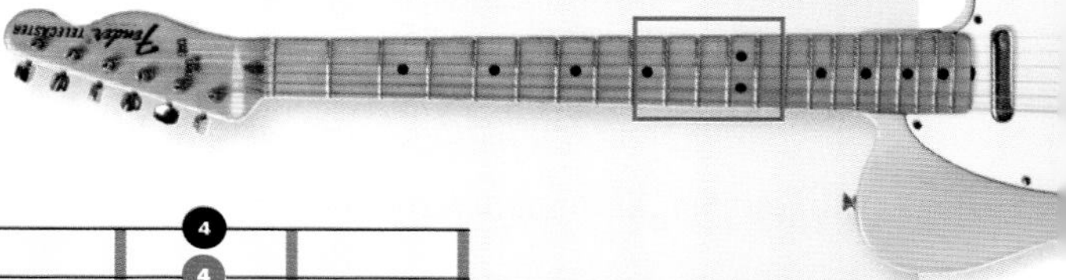

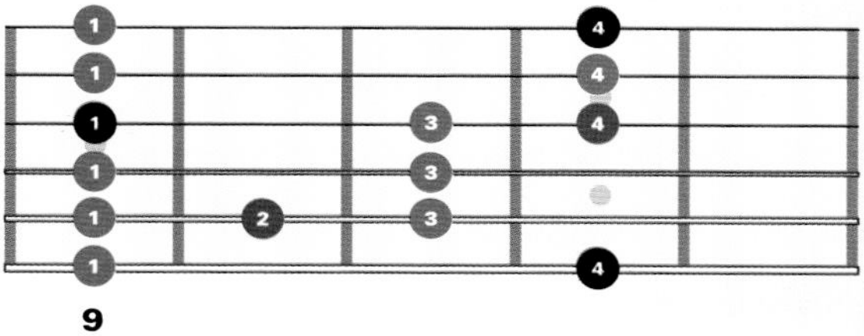

9

F major pentatonic

| R | 2 | ♯2/♭3 | 3 | 5 | 6 | OCT |

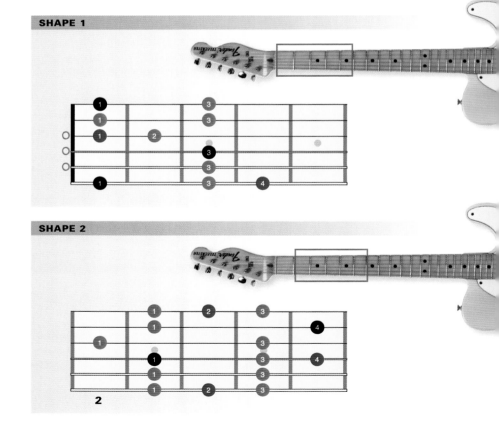

SHAPE 1

SHAPE 2

SHAPE 3

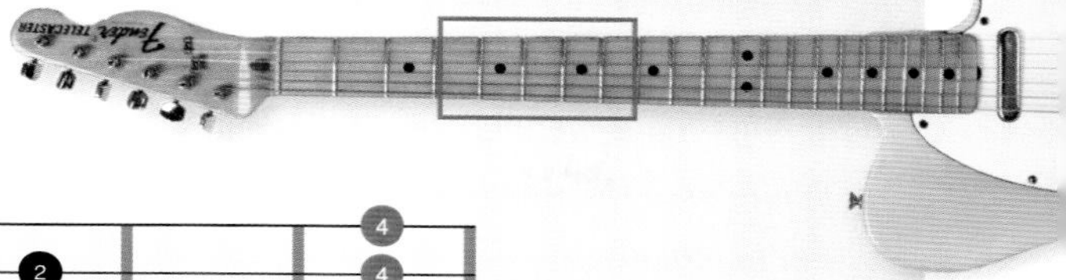

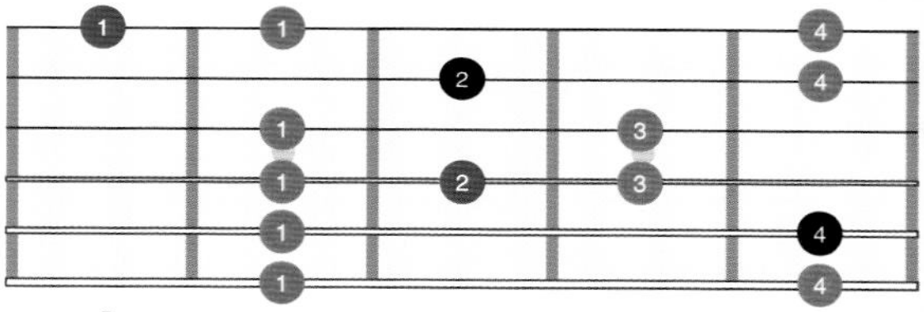

4

SHAPE 4

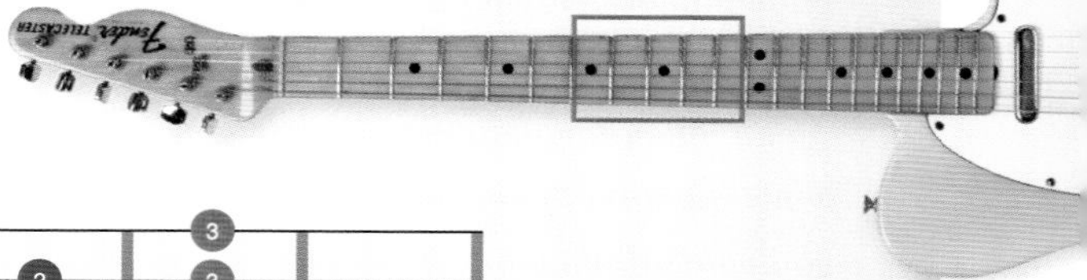

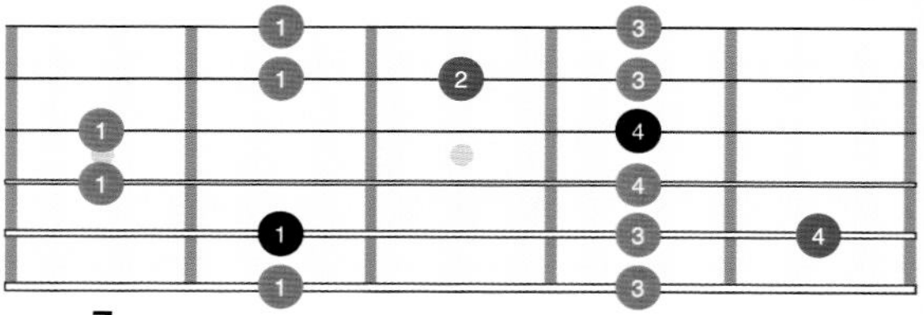

7

SHAPE 5

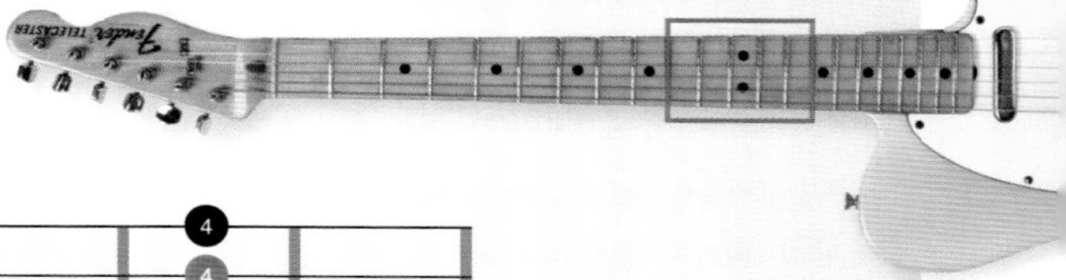

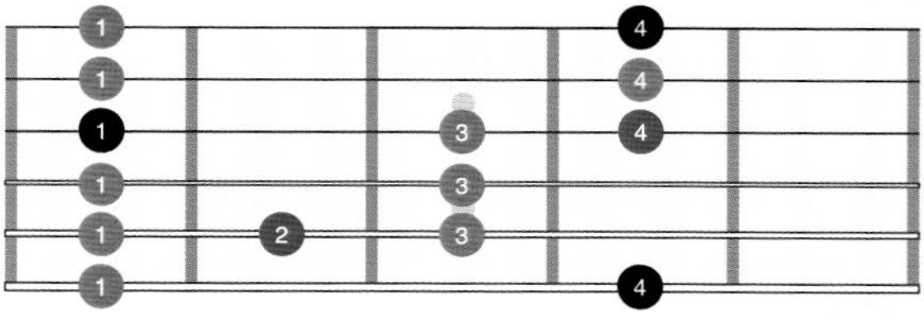

10

F♯ major pentatonic

R	2	♯2/♭3	3	5	6	OCT

SHAPE 1

SHAPE 2

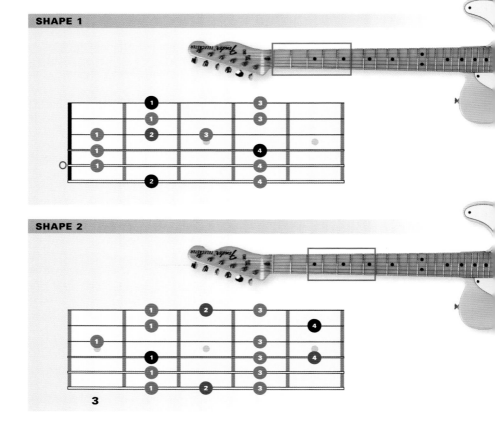

SHAPE 3

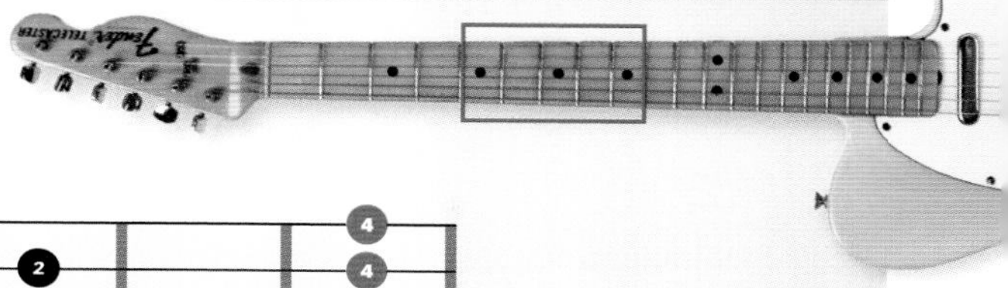

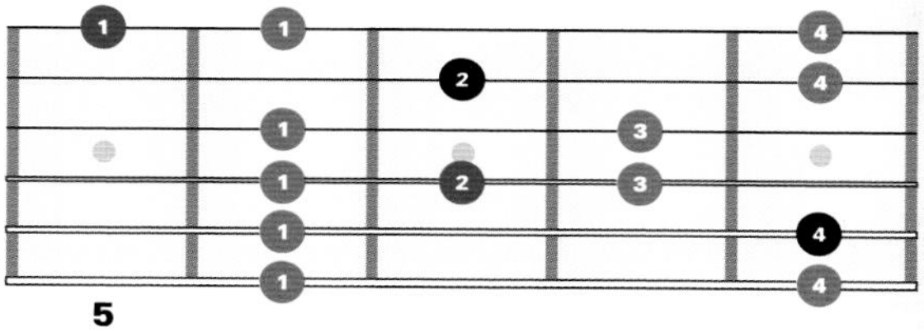

5

SHAPE 4

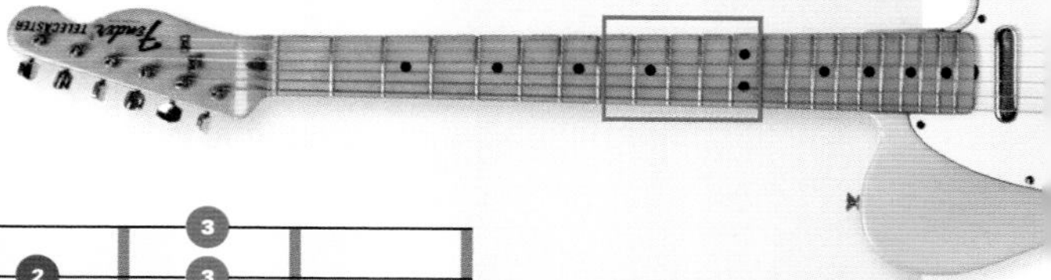

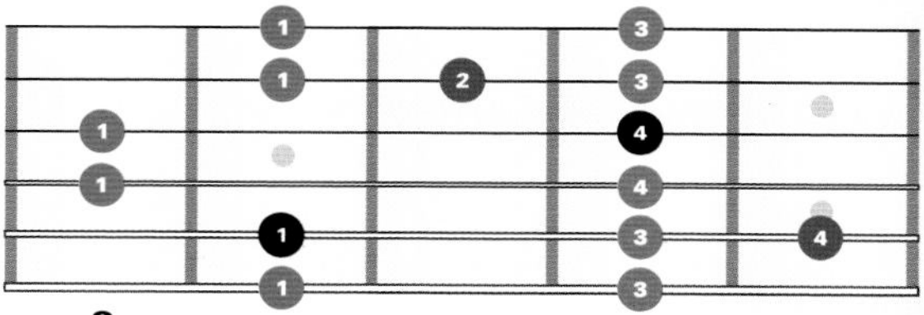

8

SHAPE 5

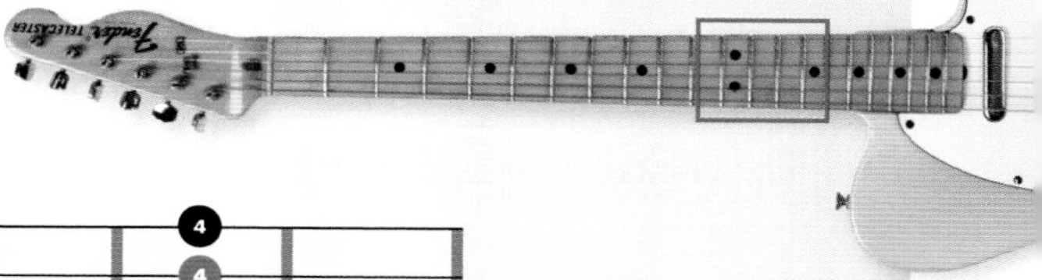

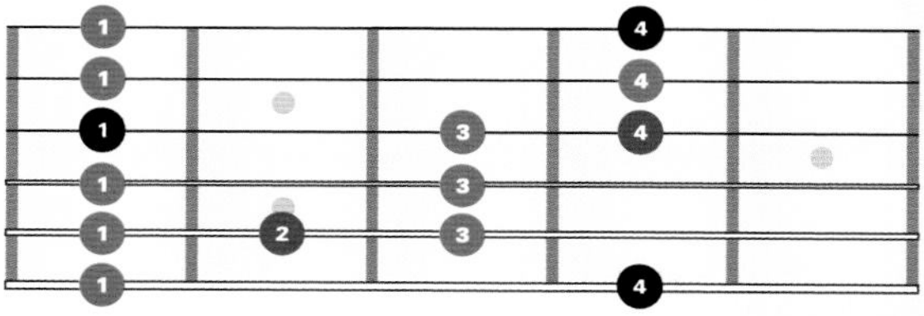

11

G major pentatonic

| R | 2 | #2/♭3 | 3 | 5 | 6 | OCT |

SHAPE 5

SHAPE 1

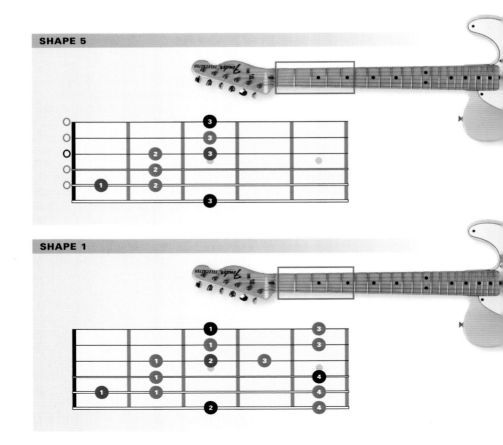

SHAPE 2

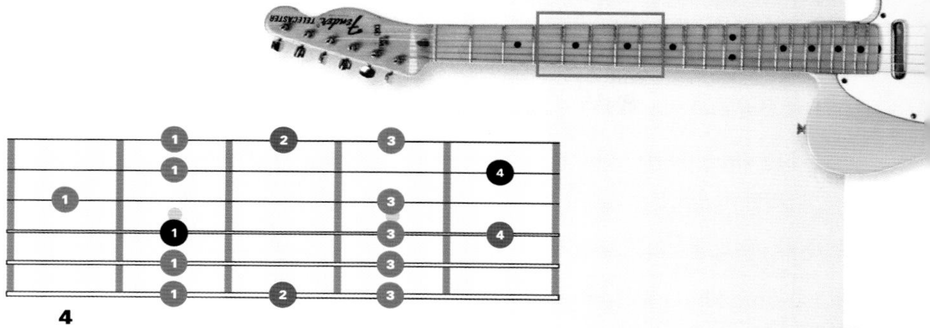

4

SHAPE 3

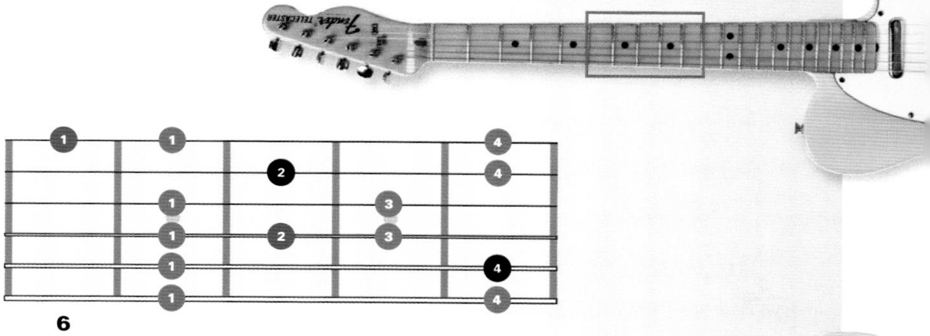

6

SHAPE 4

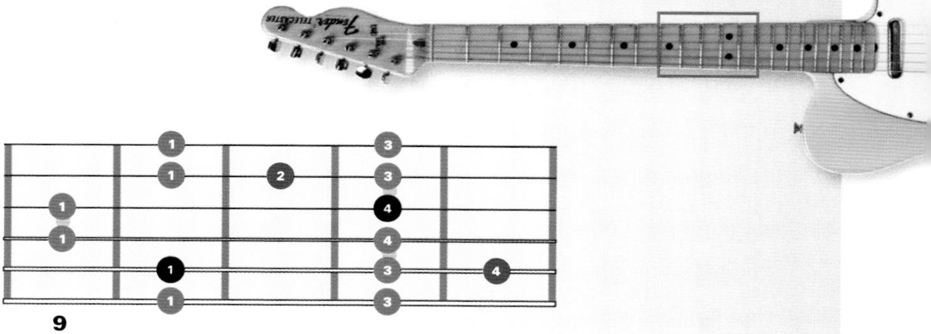

9

A♭ major pentatonic

| R | 2 | ♯2/♭3 | 3 | 5 | 6 | OCT |

SHAPE 5

SHAPE 1

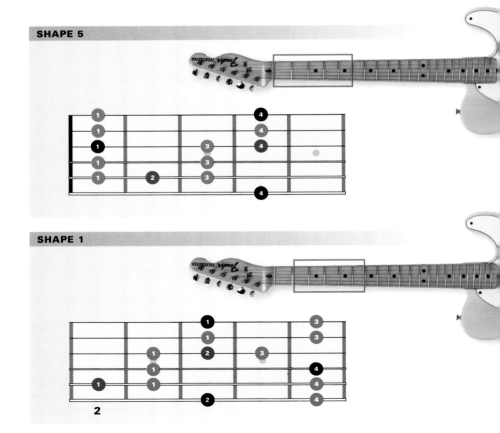

SHAPE 2

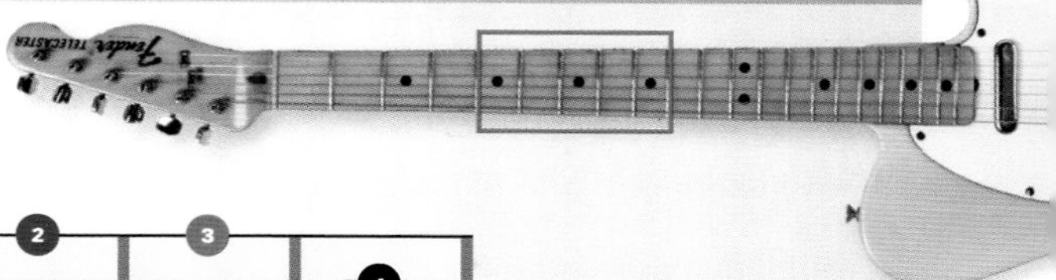

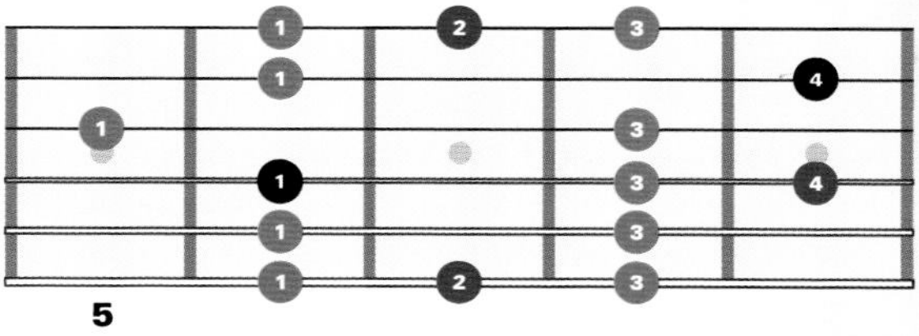

5

SHAPE 3

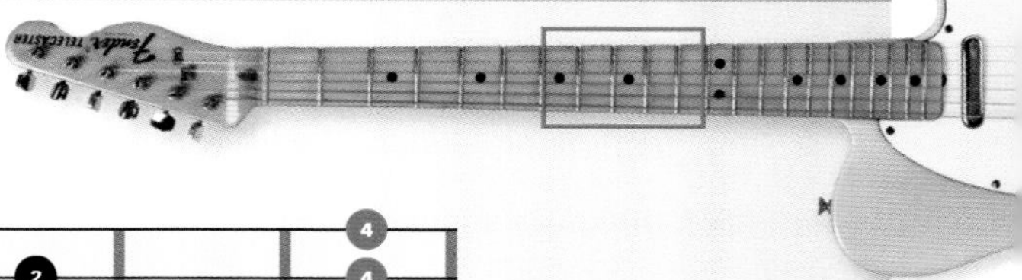

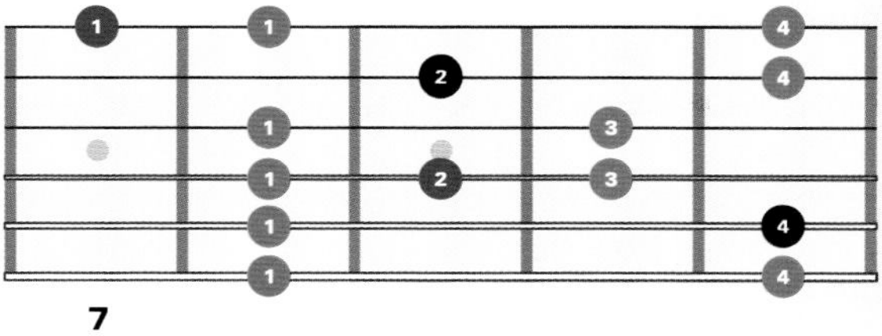

7

SHAPE 4

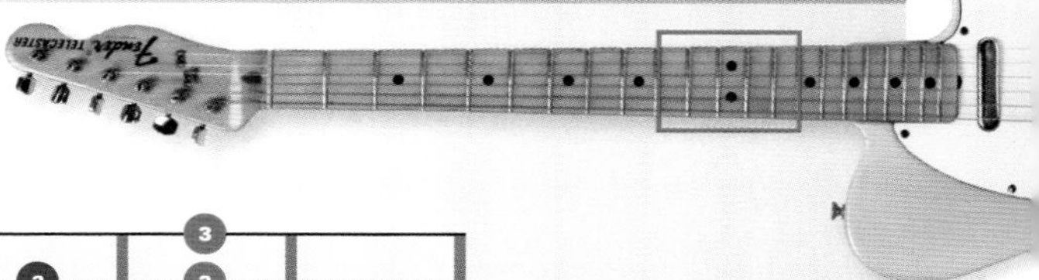

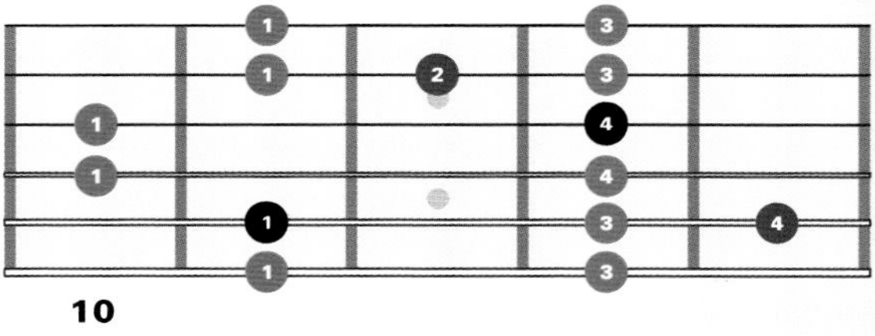

10

A major pentatonic

R	2	#2/♭3	3	5	6	OCT

SHAPE 4

SHAPE 5

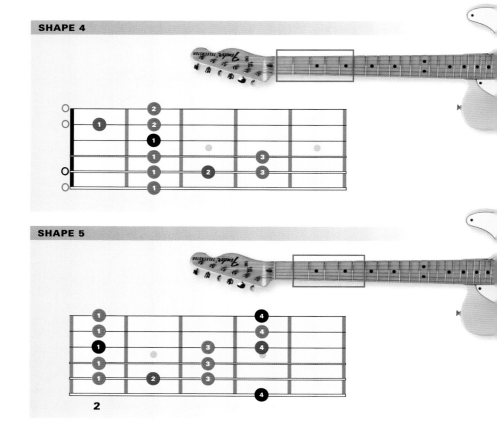

SHAPE 1

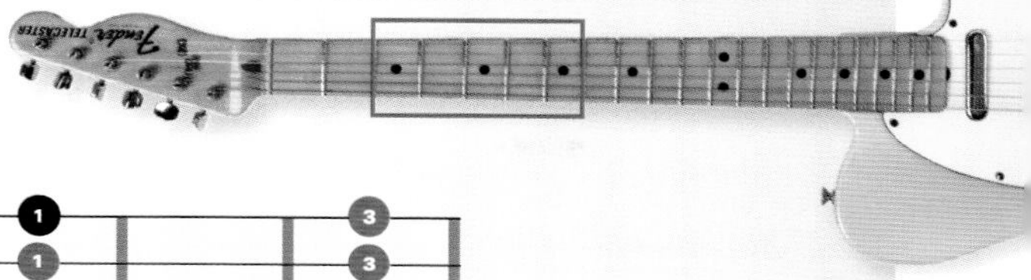

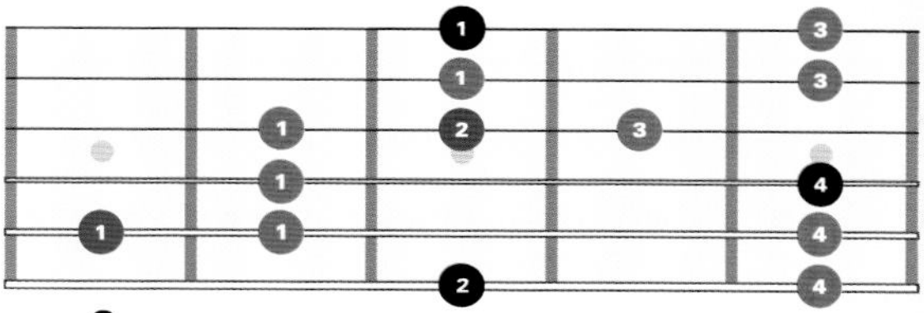

3

SHAPE 2

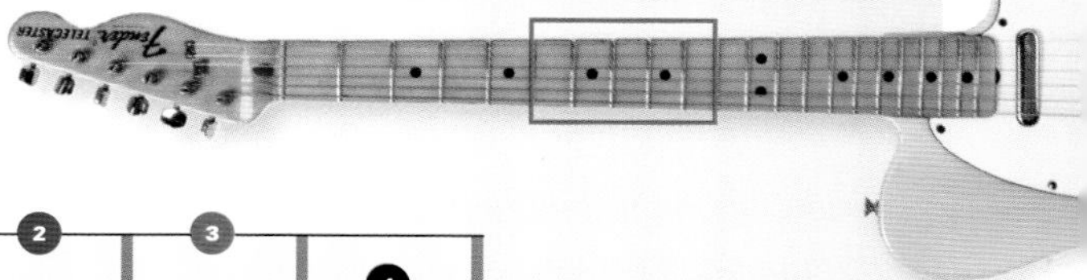

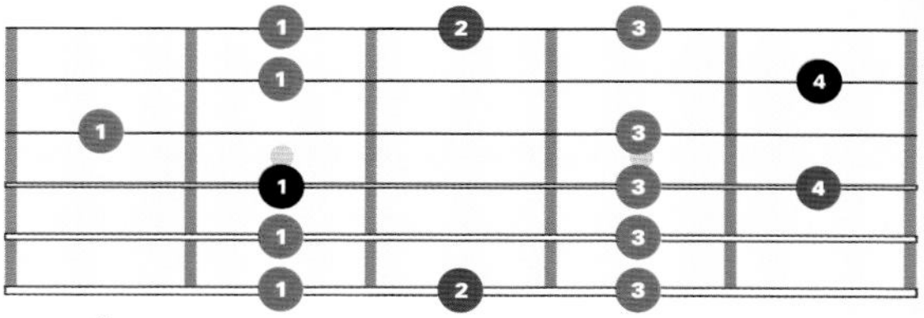

6

SHAPE 3

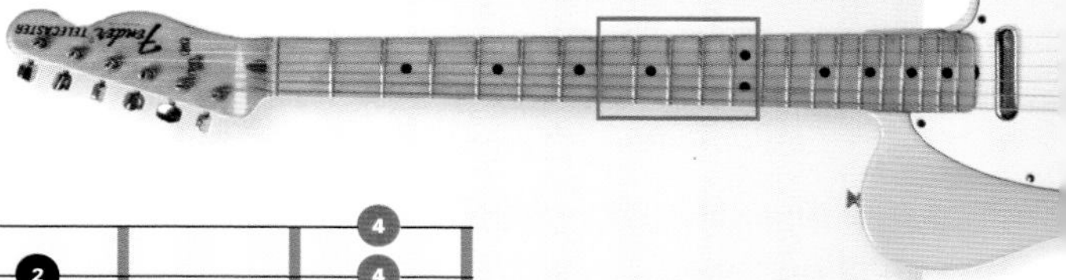

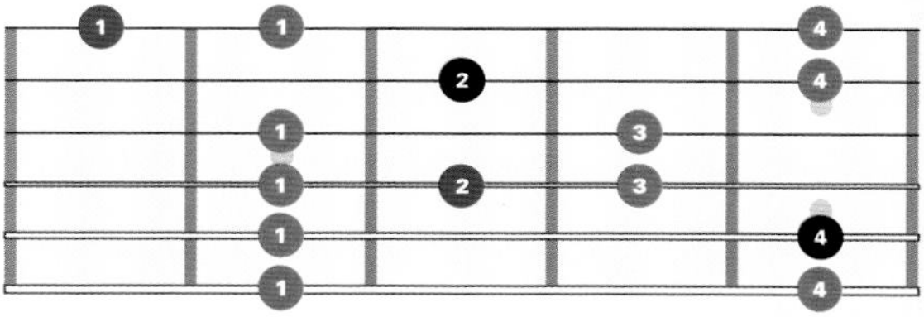

8

B♭ major pentatonic

| R | 2 | #2/♭3 | 3 | 5 | 6 | OCT |

SHAPE 4

SHAPE 5

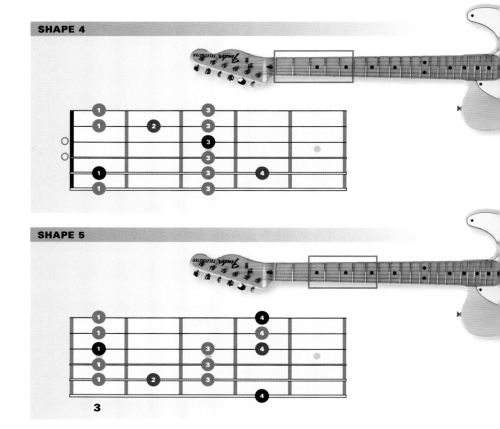

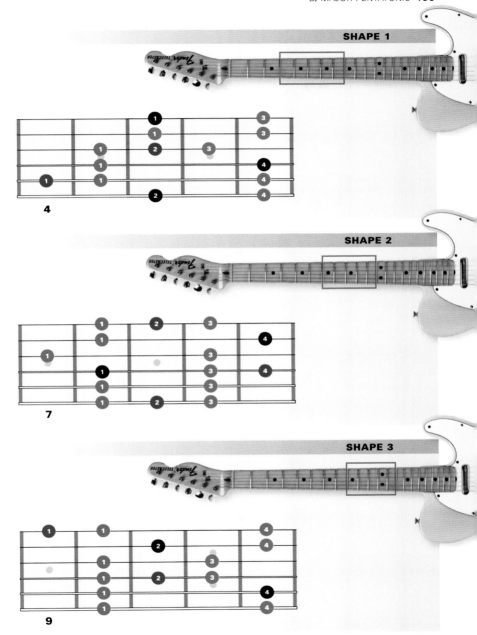

SHAPE 1

4

SHAPE 2

7

SHAPE 3

9

B major pentatonic

| R | 2 | #2/♭3 | 3 | 5 | 6 | OCT |

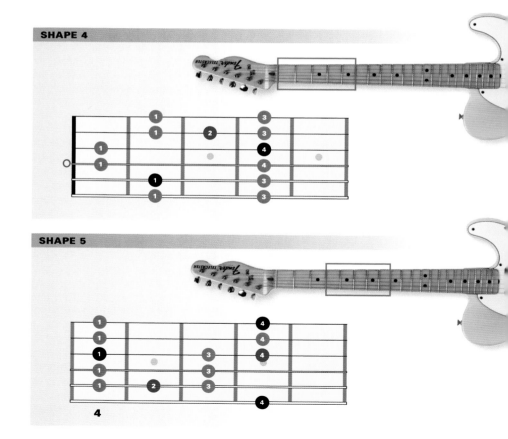

SHAPE 4

SHAPE 5

SHAPE 1

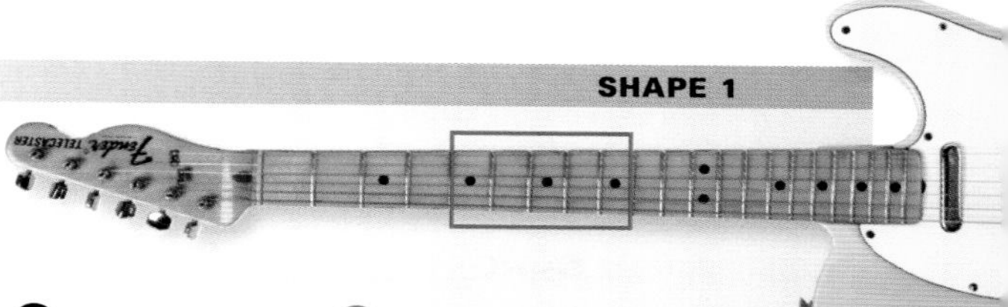

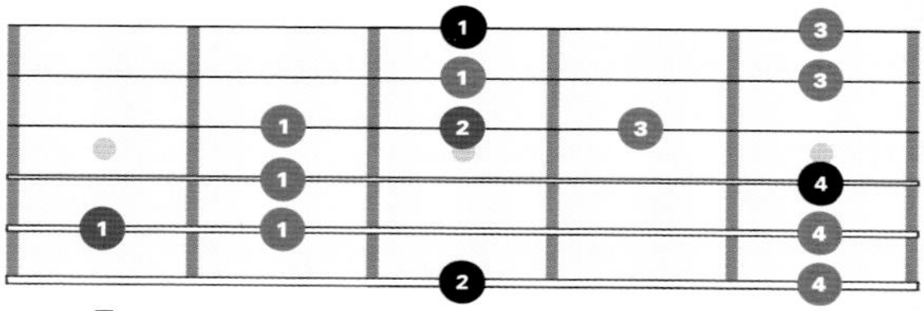

5

SHAPE 2

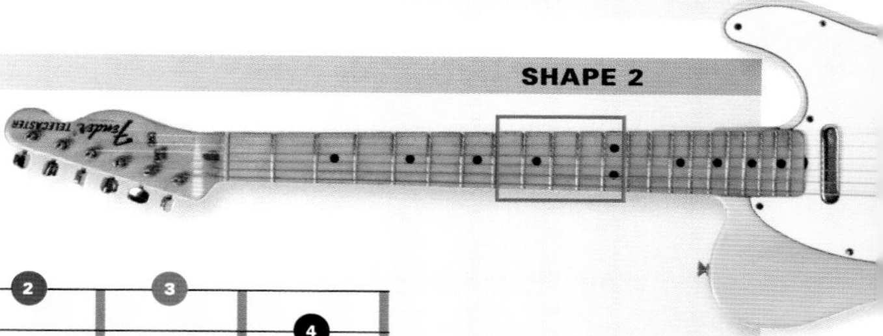

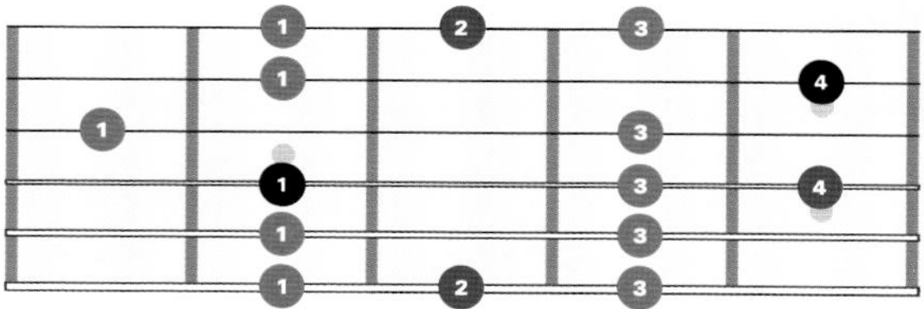

8

SHAPE 3

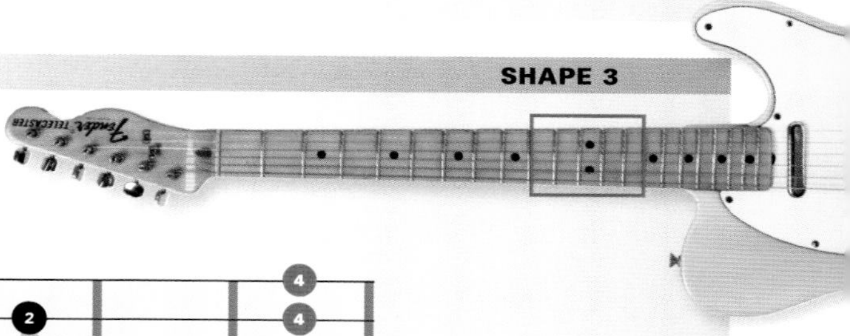

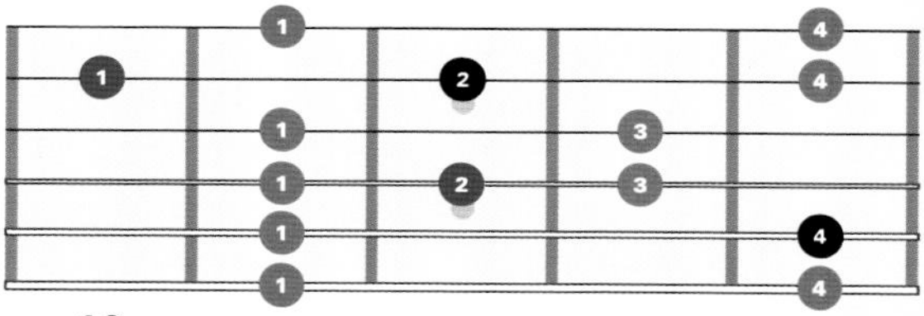

10

A minor pentatonic

| R | ♭3 | 4 | #4/♭5 | 5 | ♭7 | OCT |

SHAPE 4

SHAPE 5

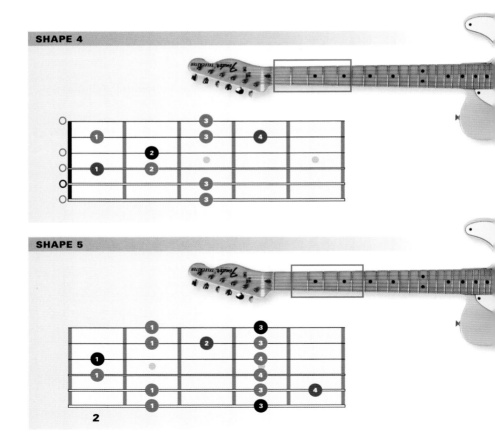

SHAPE 1

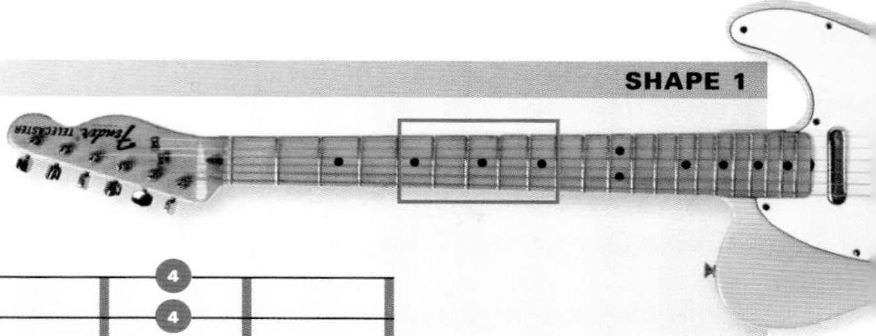

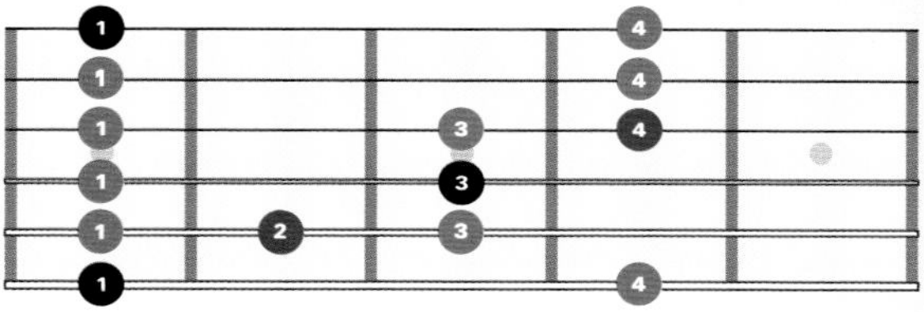

5

SHAPE 2

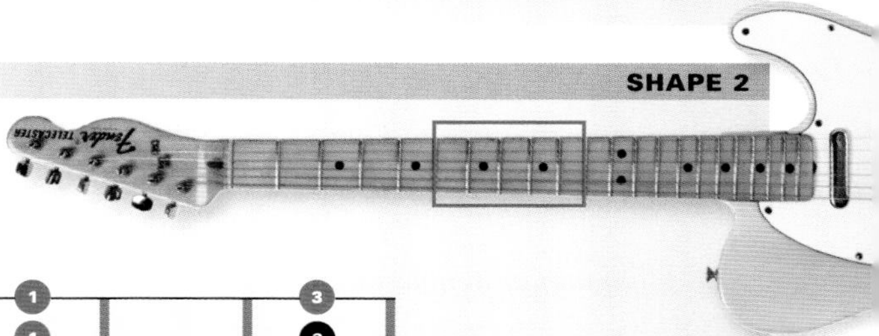

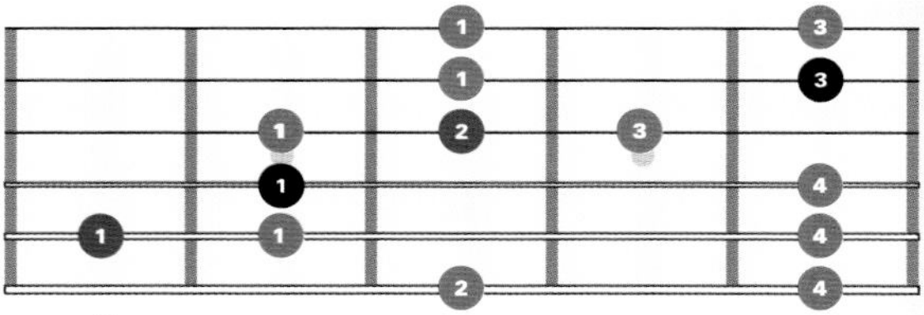

6

SHAPE 3

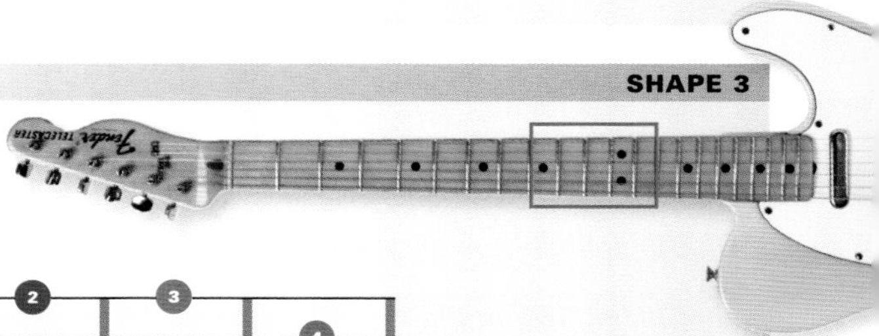

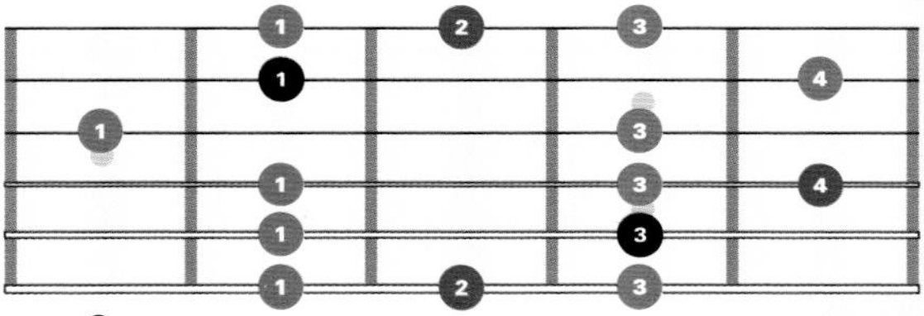

9

B♭ minor pentatonic

| R | ♭3 | 4 | #4/♭5 | 5 | ♭7 | OCT |

SHAPE 4

SHAPE 5

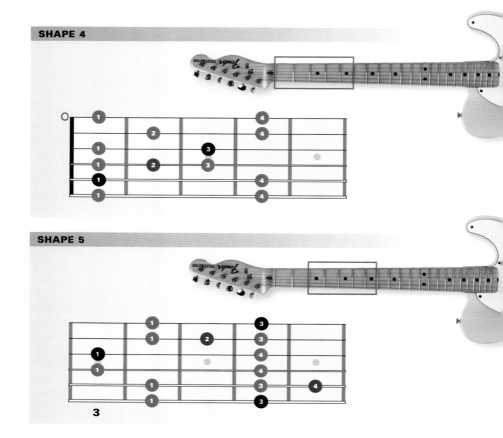

SHAPE 1

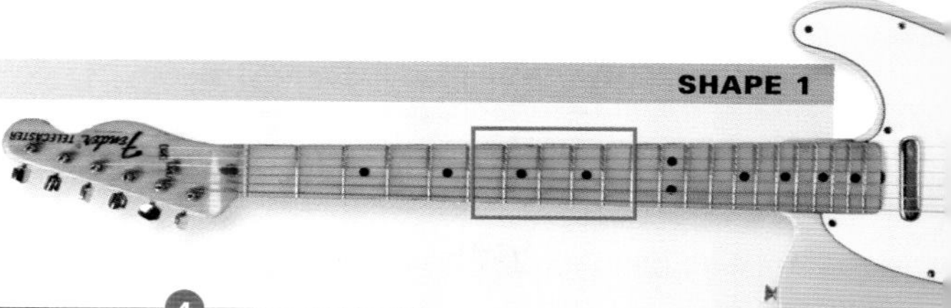

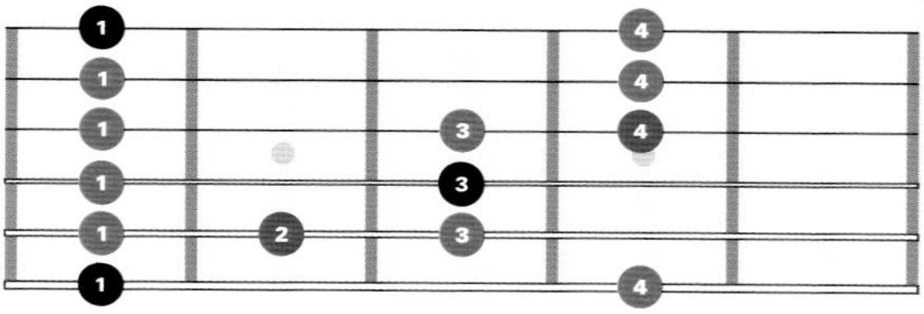

6

SHAPE 2

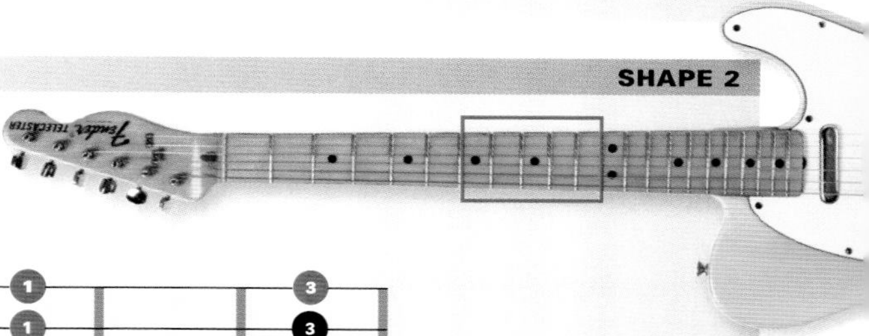

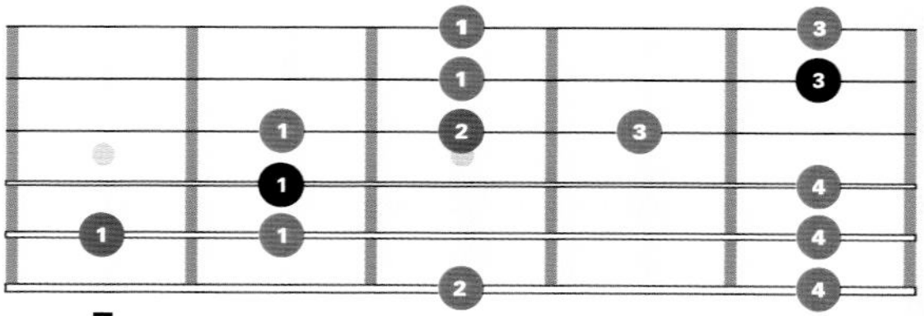

7

SHAPE 3

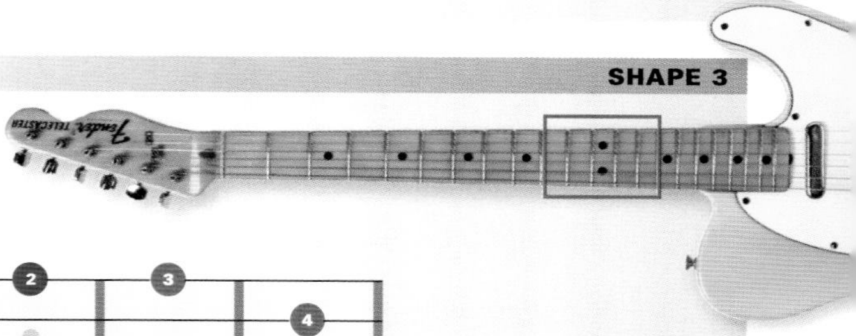

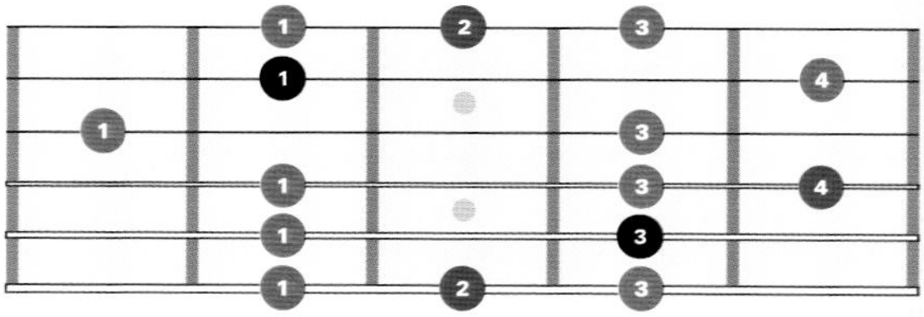

10

B minor pentatonic

| R | ♭3 | 4 | ♯4/♭5 | 5 | ♭7 | OCT |

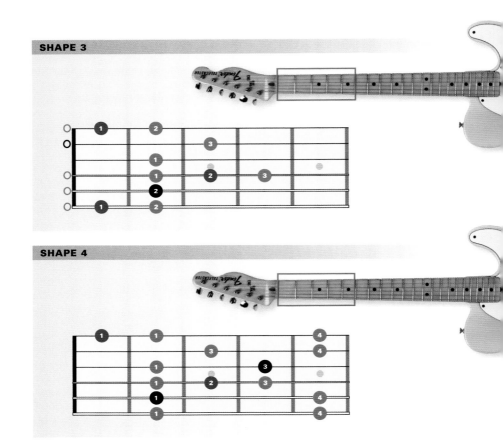

SHAPE 5

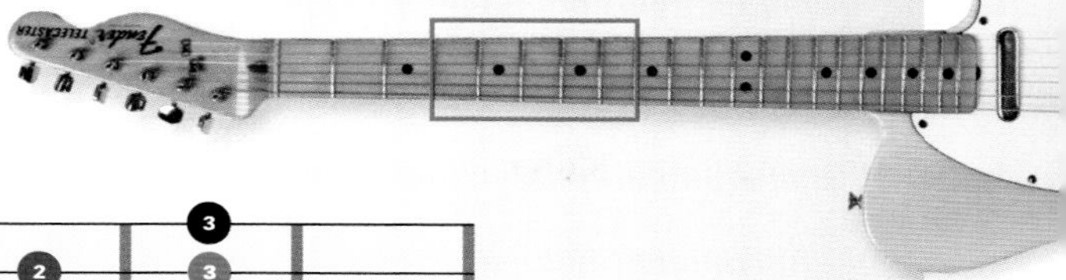

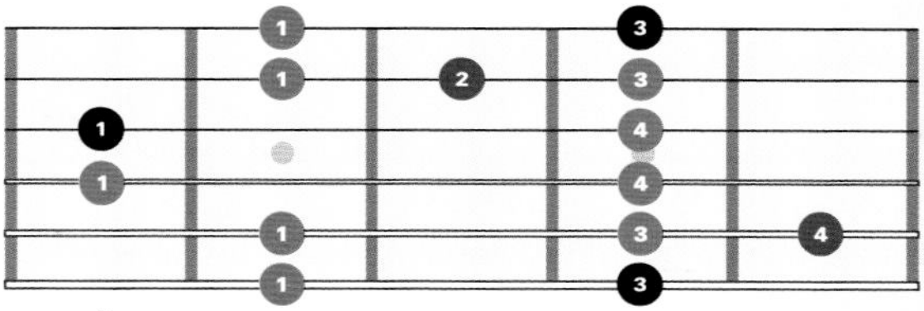

4

SHAPE 1

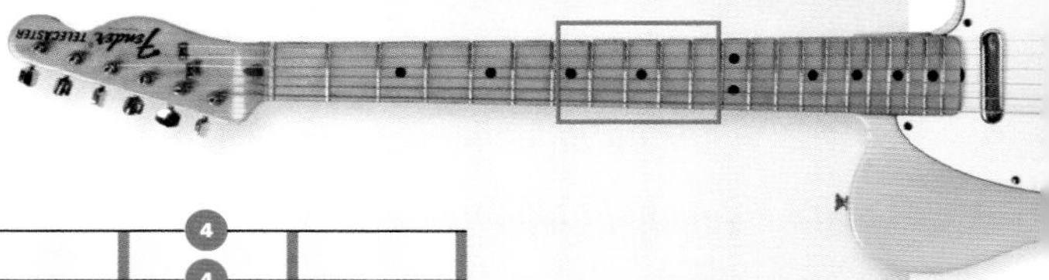

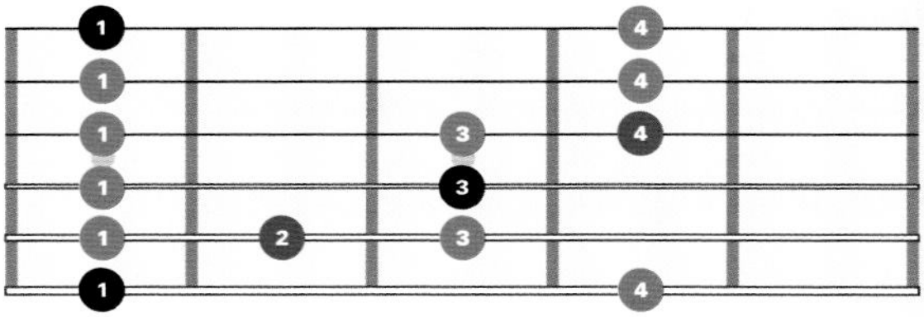

7

SHAPE 2

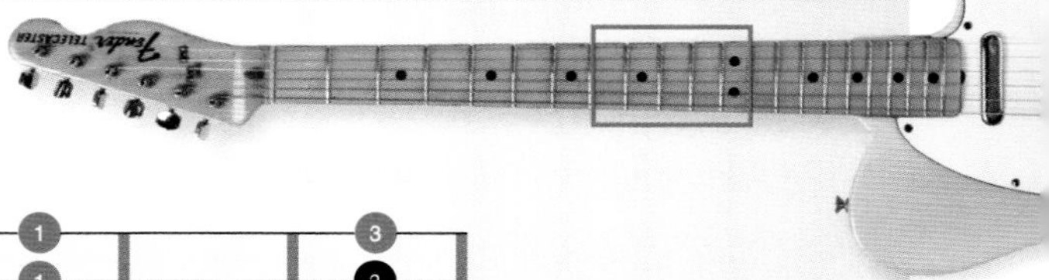

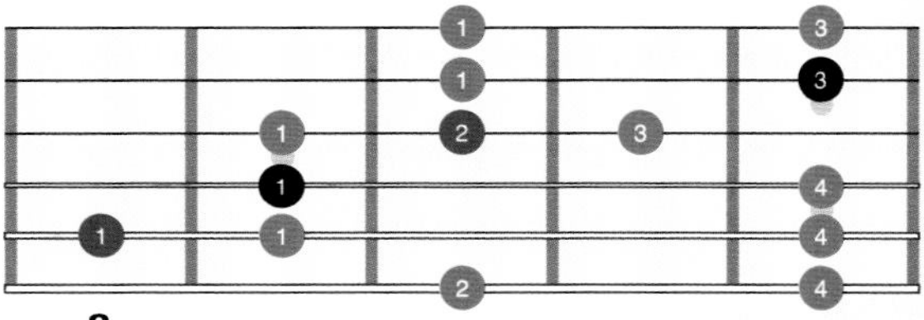

8

C minor pentatonic

| R | ♭3 | 4 | ♯4/♭5 | 5 | ♭7 | OCT |

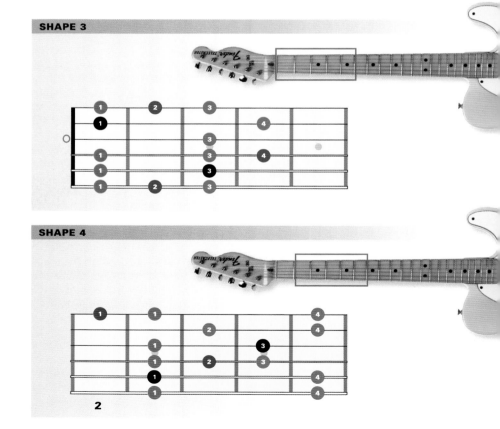

SHAPE 3

SHAPE 4

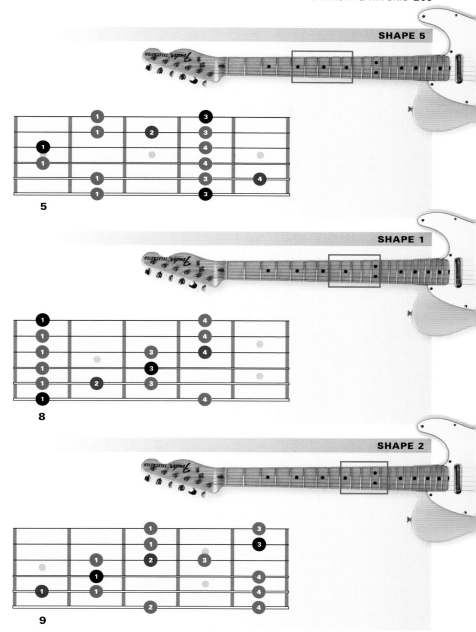

SHAPE 5

5

SHAPE 1

8

SHAPE 2

9

C# minor pentatonic

| R | ♭3 | 4 | #4/♭5 | 5 | ♭7 | OCT |

SHAPE 3

SHAPE 4

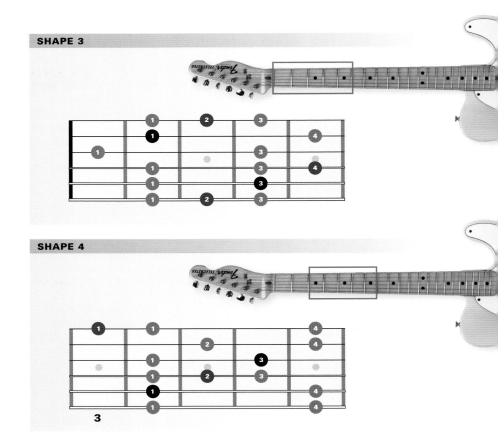

SHAPE 5

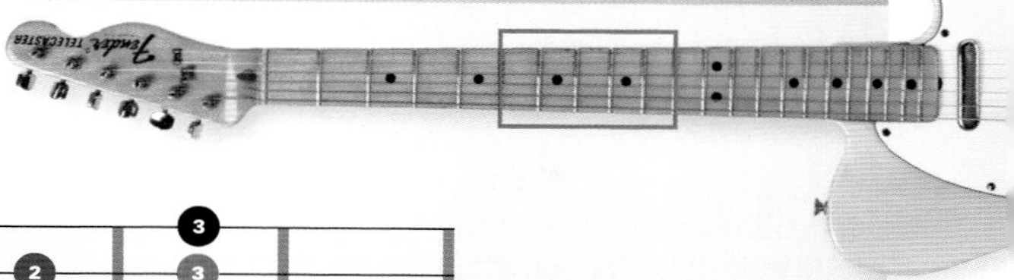

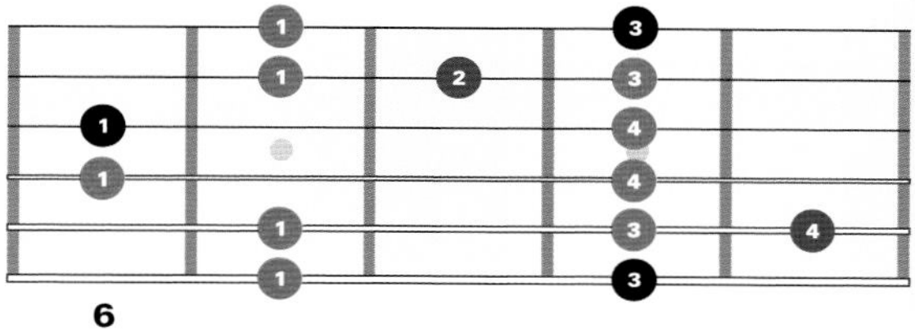

6

SHAPE 1

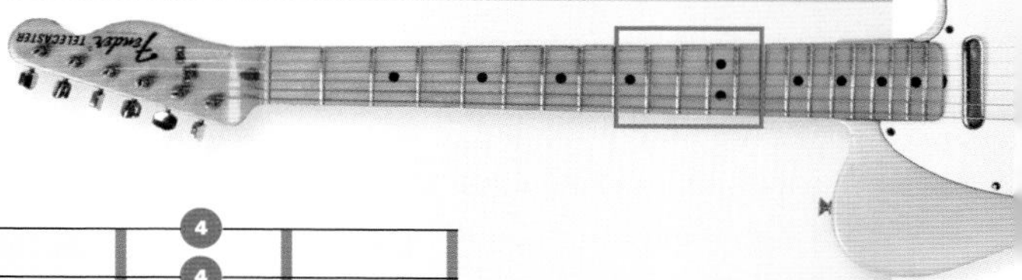

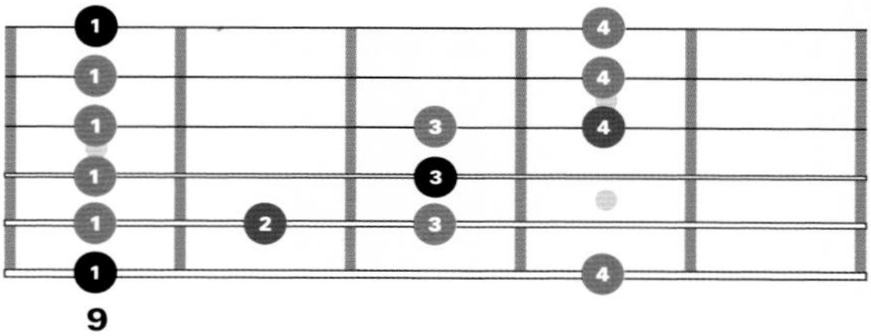

9

SHAPE 2

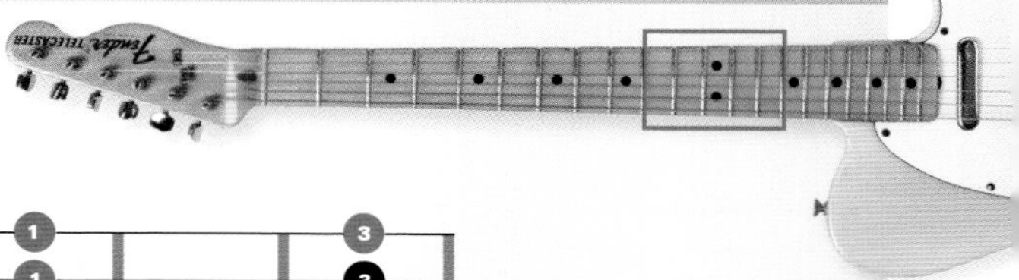

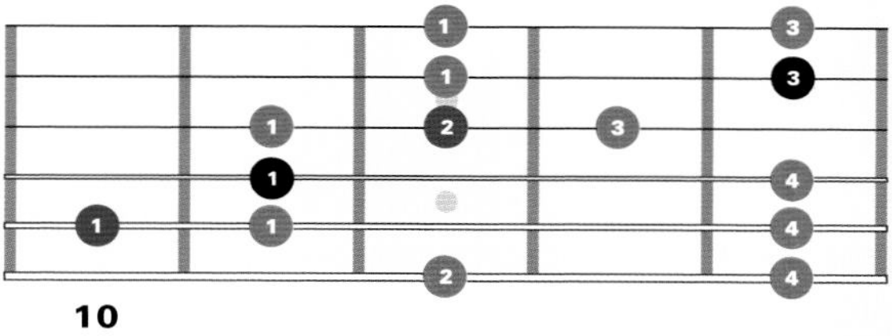

10

D minor pentatonic

| R | ♭3 | 4 | ♯4/♭5 | 5 | ♭7 | OCT |

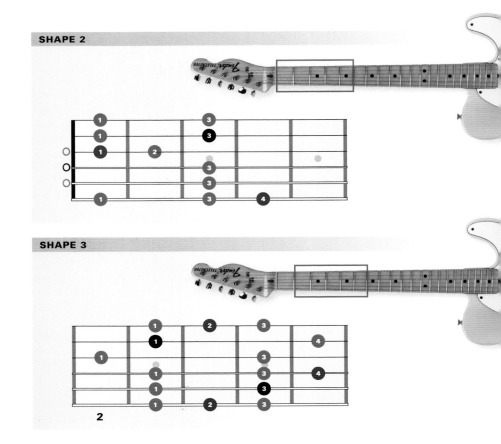

SHAPE 2

SHAPE 3

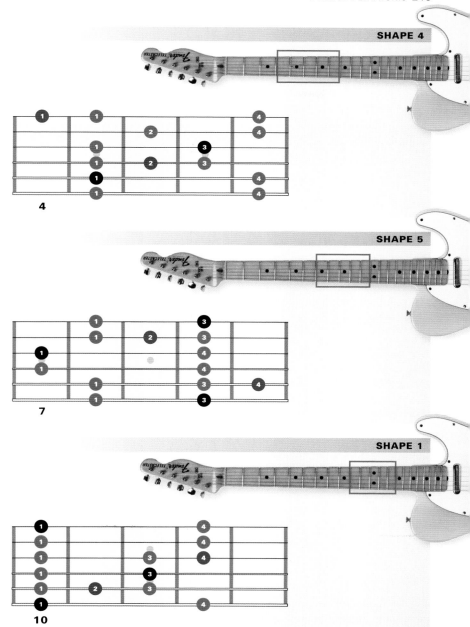

E♭ minor pentatonic

R	♭3	4	♯4/♭5	5	♭7	OCT

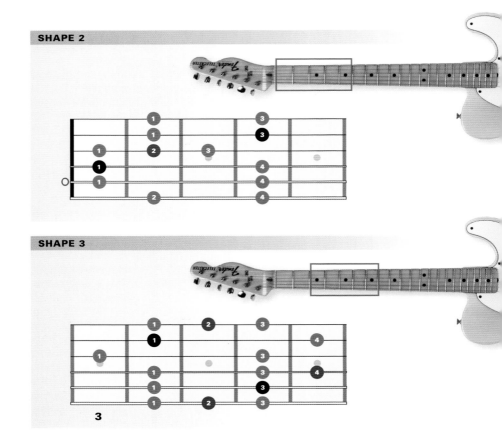

SHAPE 4

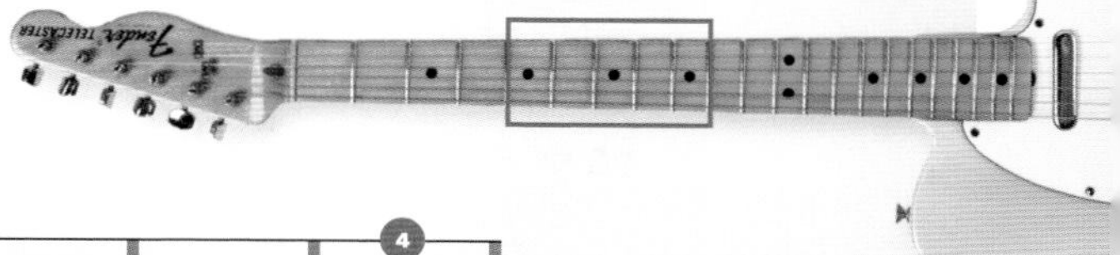

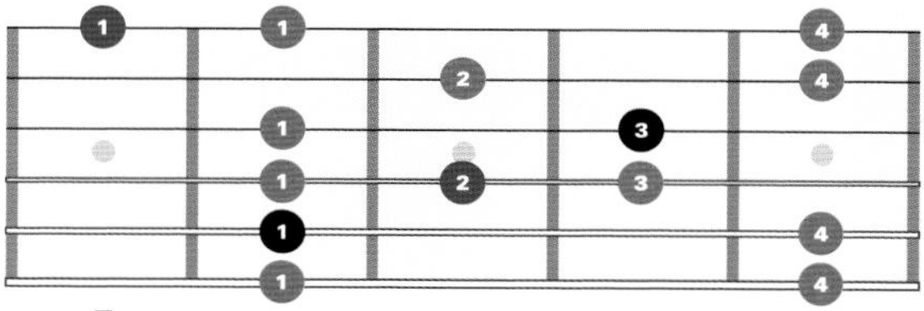

5

SHAPE 5

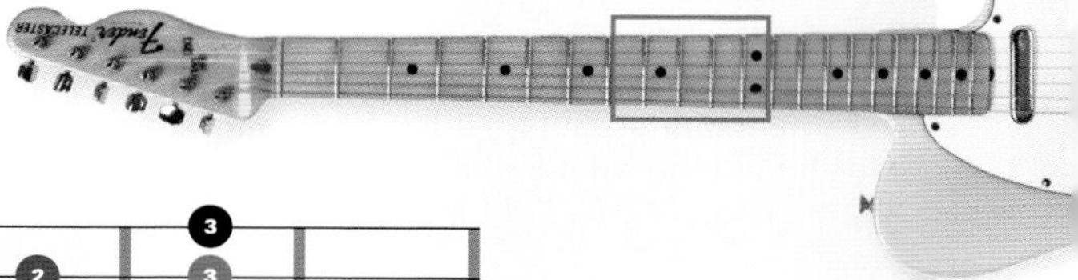

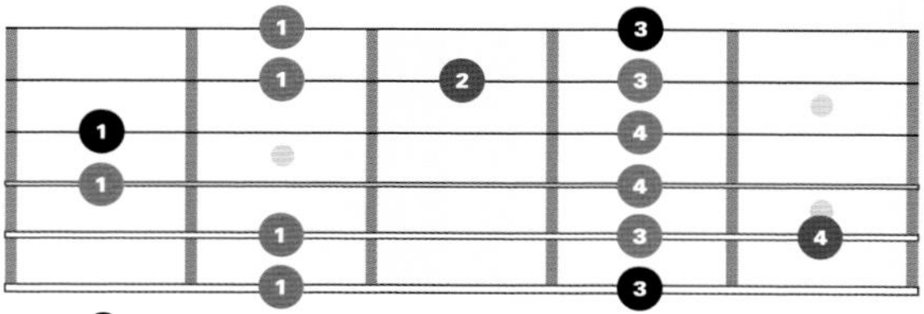

8

SHAPE 1

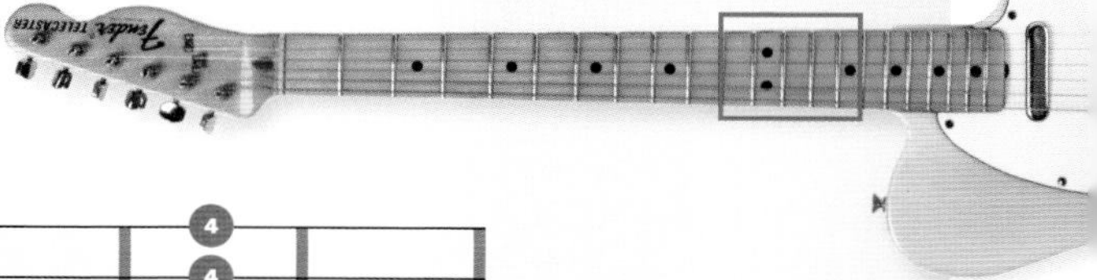

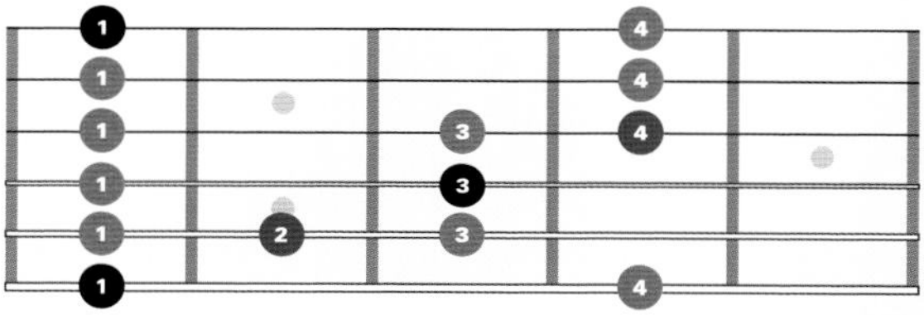

11

E minor pentatonic

| R | ♭3 | 4 | ♯4/♭5 | 5 | ♭7 | OCT |

SHAPE 1

SHAPE 2

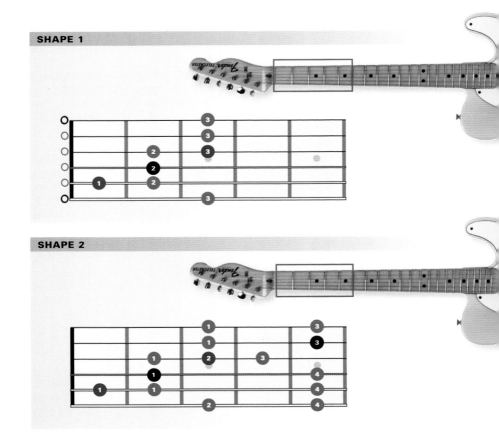

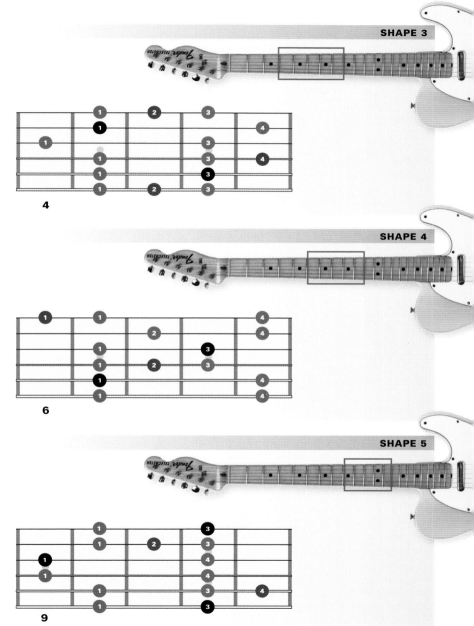

F minor pentatonic

R   ♭3   4   ♯4/♭5   5   ♭7   OCT

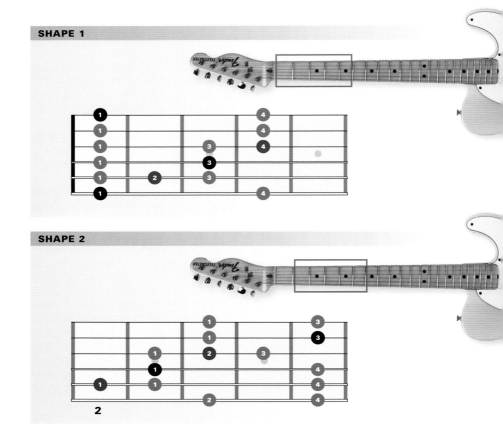

SHAPE 1

SHAPE 2

SHAPE 3

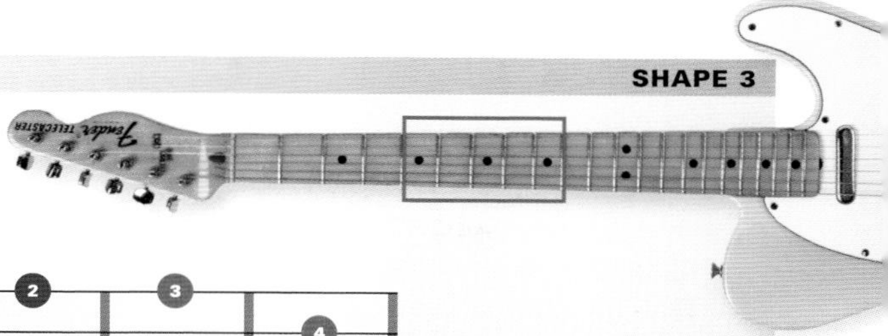

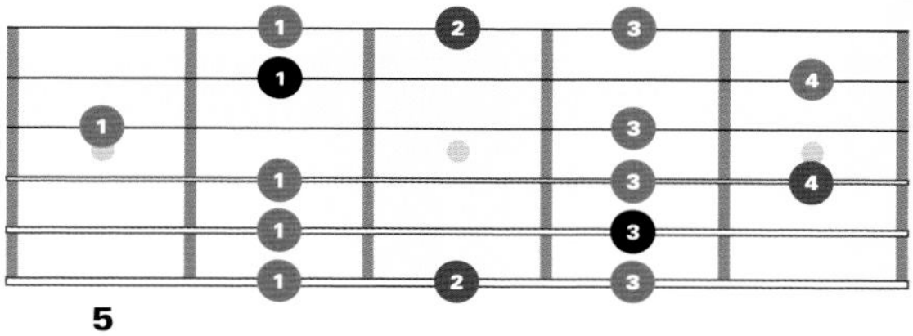

5

SHAPE 4

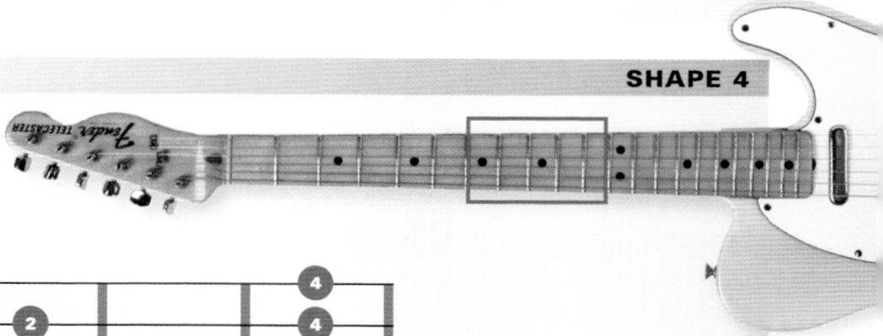

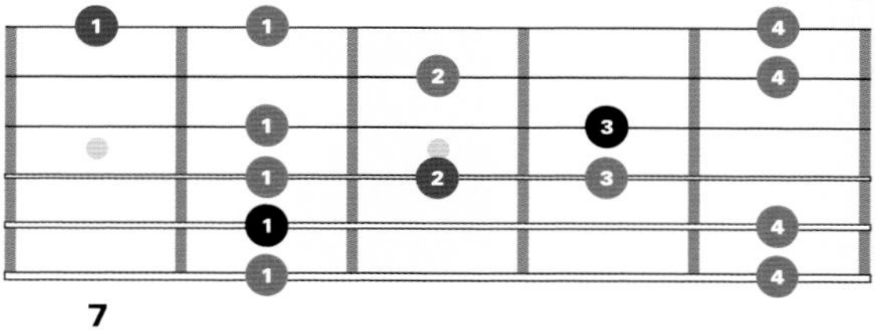

7

SHAPE 5

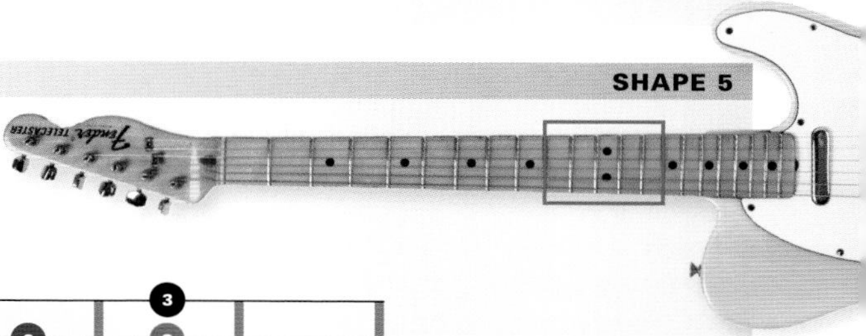

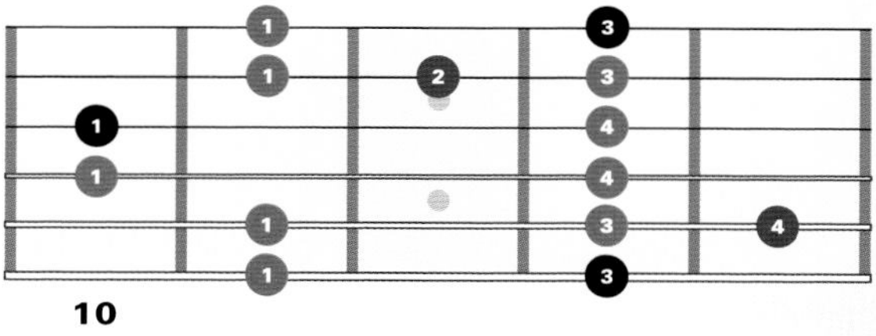

10

F# minor pentatonic

| R | ♭3 | 4 | ♯4/♭5 | 5 | ♭7 | OCT |

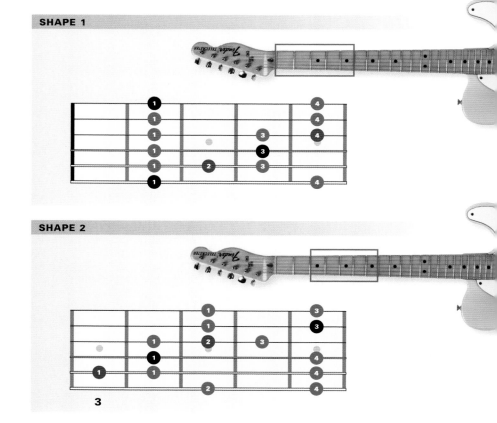

SHAPE 1

SHAPE 2

3

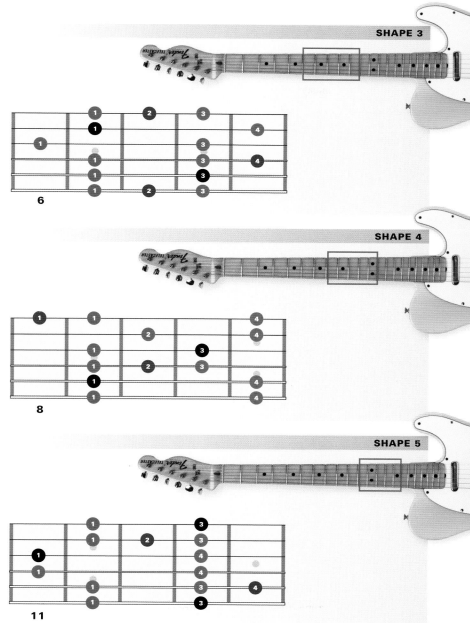

SHAPE 3

6

SHAPE 4

8

SHAPE 5

11

G minor pentatonic

| R | ♭3 | 4 | ♯4/♭5 | 5 | ♭7 | OCT |

SHAPE 5

SHAPE 1

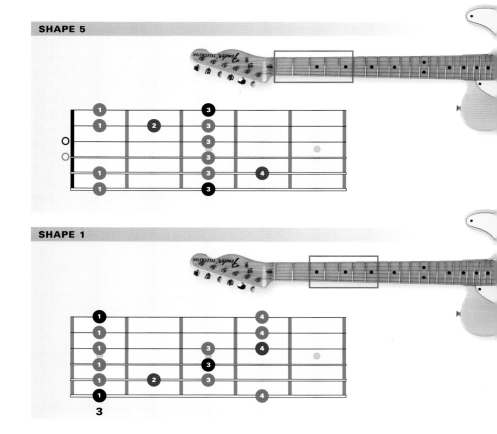

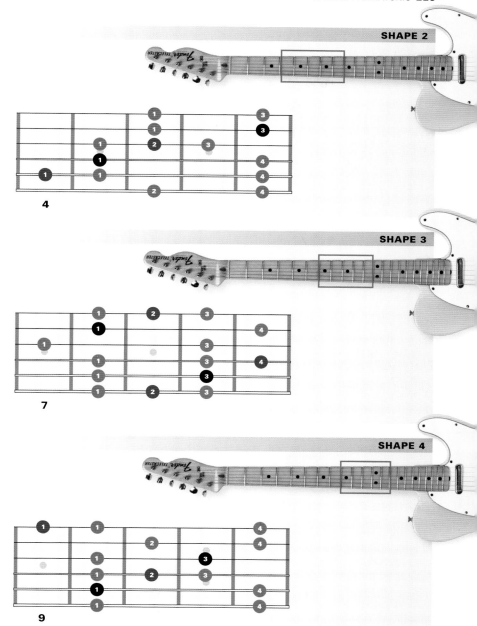

SHAPE 2

4

SHAPE 3

7

SHAPE 4

9

G♯ minor pentatonic

| R | ♭3 | 4 | ♯4/♭5 | 5 | ♭7 | OCT |

SHAPE 5

SHAPE 1

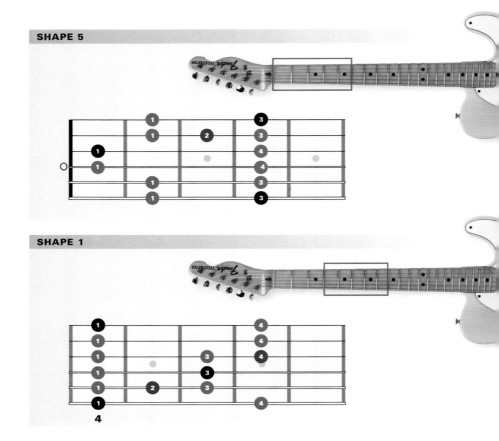

SHAPE 2

5

SHAPE 3

8

SHAPE 4

10

OPEN TUNING SCALE LIBRARY

Notation guide

Open position (first fret) scale box:

Scale box starting at the seventh fret:

7

✖ open string *not* played

○ open string (root note) played

○ open string (chord note) played

● root note

● scale note

● "blue" note

CHAPTER 4

One of the things that often deters potential slide players is the prospect of learning a whole new set of scale patterns. But this is not as daunting as it sounds because open tuning converts the guitar to a single, open-chord shape, making the CAGED system redundant. So, in this section, you'll find just two shapes for every scale. Shape one is based around the tonic major chord that forms a straight line across the frets (i.e. fifth string root note in open G and sixth string root note in open D). Shape two simply slots in front of shape one to form a twelve-fret "super shape," mapping the entire fingerboard with a single pentatonic scale.

Every note has also been color-coded in exactly the same way as in the previous section (see key opposite), making it easy to identify the root notes and "blue" notes. As before, aim to practice each pattern with and without the "blue" notes to improve your ear, your technique, and ultimately your improvising skills. This resource will enable you to overcome the problems of playing in open tuning quickly and logically, leaving you free to create those super-cool slide licks and solos!

PRACTICE TIPS

- Practice the scale shapes both horizontally and vertically, making sure you damp the surrounding strings carefully.

- Learn the available open strings in every key. These notes not only facilitate easy position shifts, but they also sound great when alternated with slide notes.

- Don't forget to also damp behind the slide. If you're wearing the slide on your third finger, then you can place your first and second fingers behind it, laying them gently across the strings.

Open G tuning

C major pentatonic

SHAPE 1

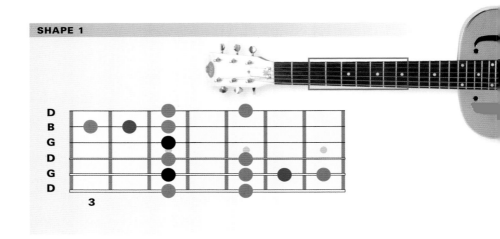

SHAPE 2

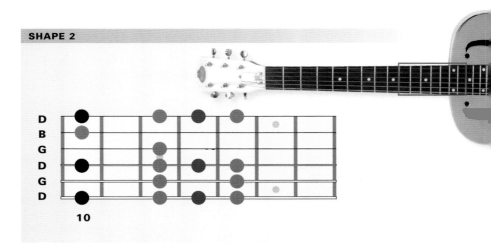

Open G tuning

C# major pentatonic

SHAPE 1

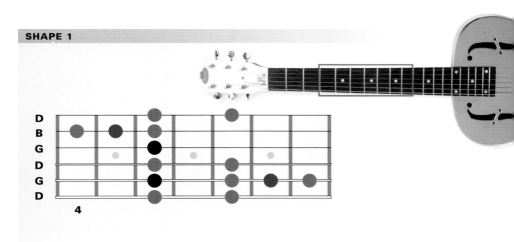

SHAPE 2

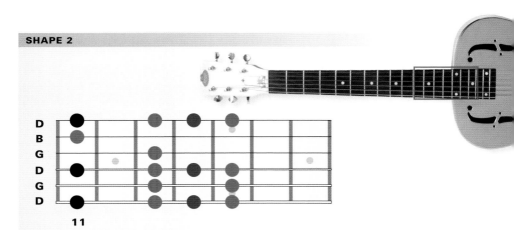

Open G tuning

D major pentatonic

SHAPE 2

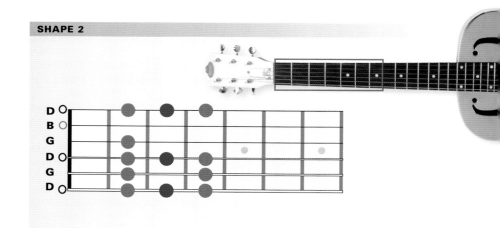

SHAPE 1

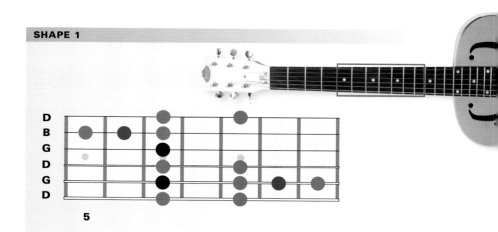

Open G tuning

E♭ major pentatonic

SHAPE 2

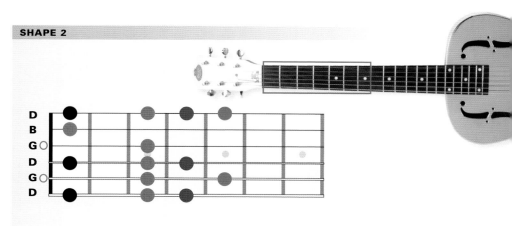

SHAPE 1

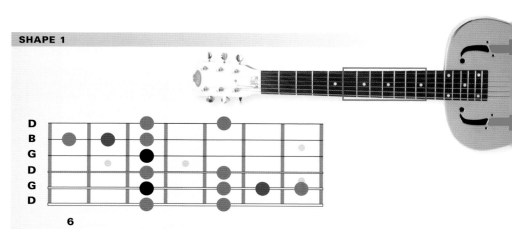

Open G tuning

E major pentatonic

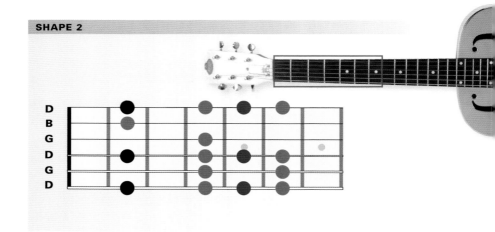

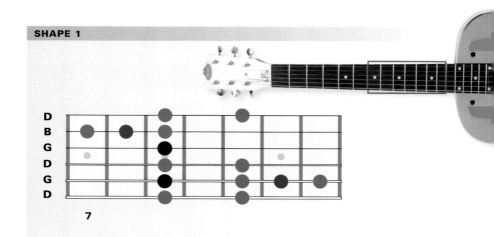

Open G tuning

F major pentatonic

SHAPE 2

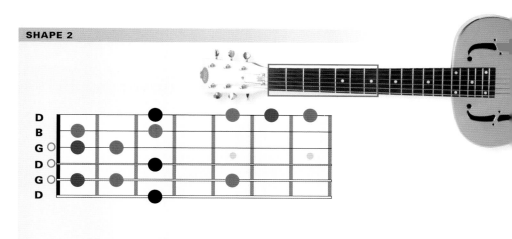

SHAPE 1

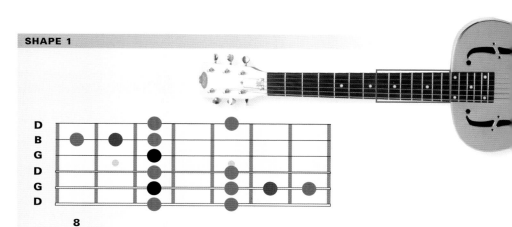

Open G tuning

F# major pentatonic

SHAPE 2

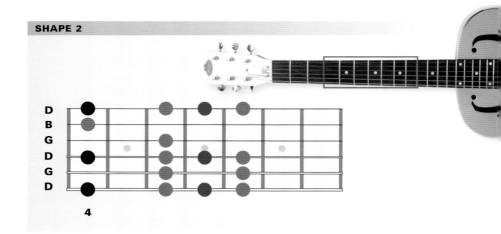

SHAPE 1

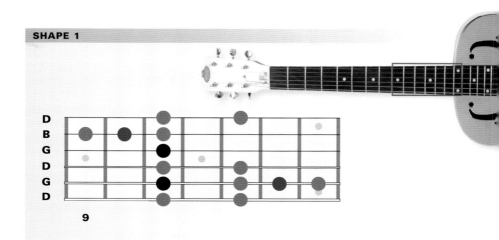

Open G tuning

G major pentatonic

SHAPE 1

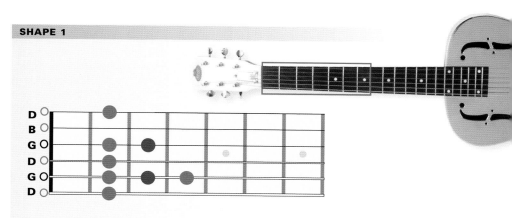

SHAPE 2

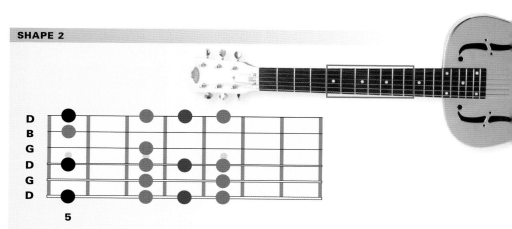

Open G tuning

A♭ major pentatonic

SHAPE 1

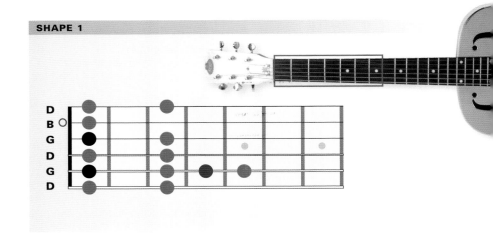

SHAPE 2

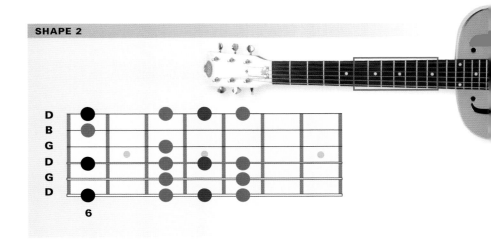

A major pentatonic

SHAPE 1

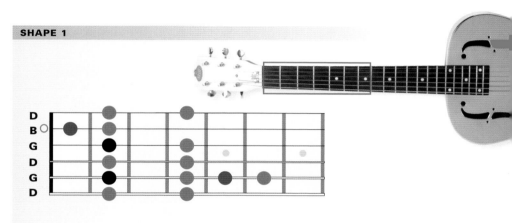

SHAPE 2

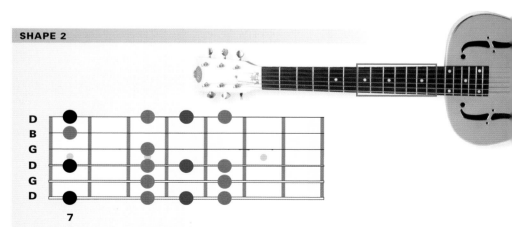

Open G tuning

B♭ major pentatonic

SHAPE 1

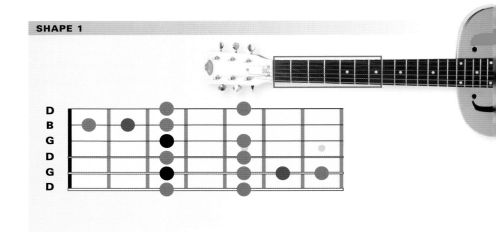

SHAPE 2

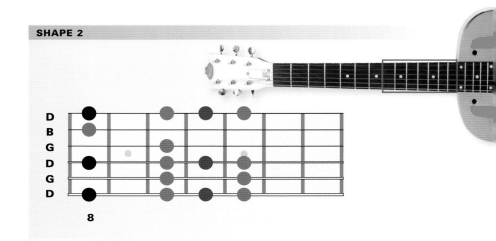

Open G tuning

B major pentatonic

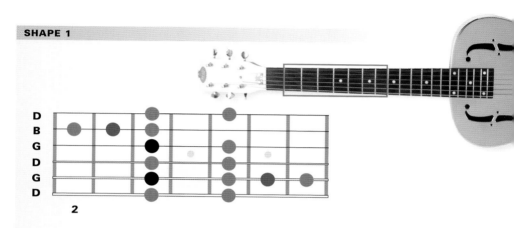

SHAPE 1

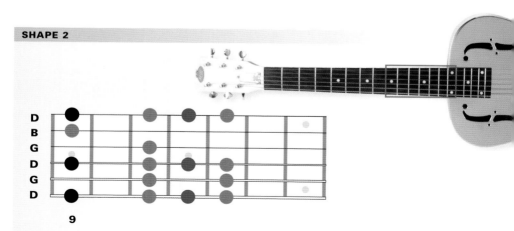

SHAPE 2

Open D tuning

C major pentatonic

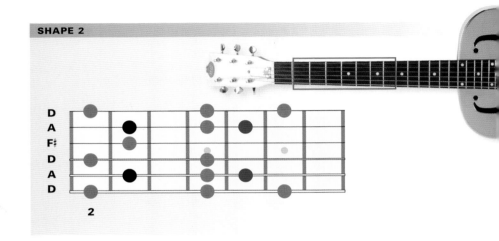

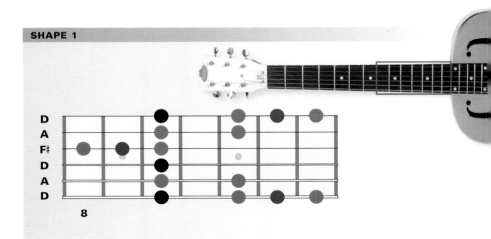

Open D tuning

C# major pentatonic

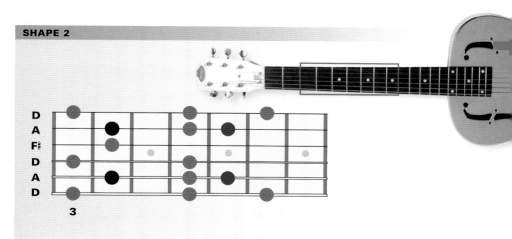

SHAPE 2

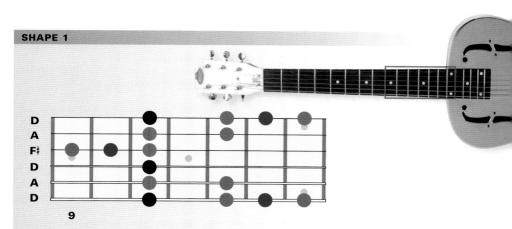

SHAPE 1

Open D tuning

D major pentatonic

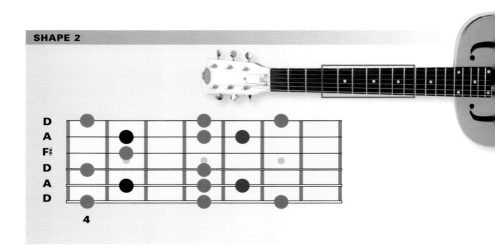

Eb major pentatonic

SHAPE 1

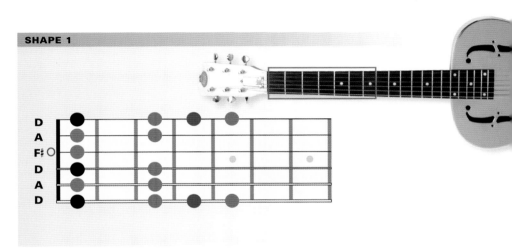

SHAPE 2

Open D tuning

E major pentatonic

SHAPE 1

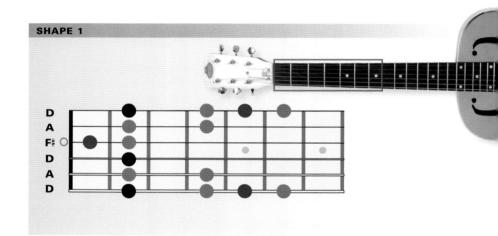

SHAPE 2

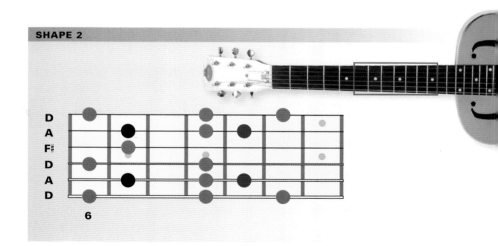

Open D tuning

F major pentatonic

SHAPE 1

SHAPE 2

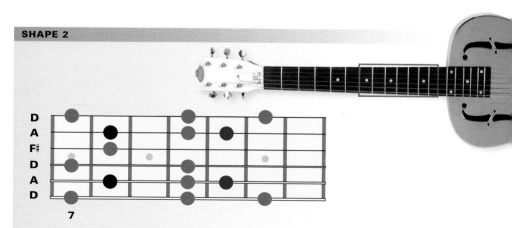

Open D tuning

F# major pentatonic

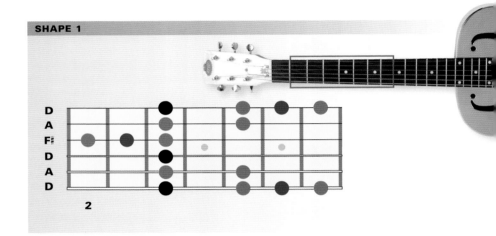

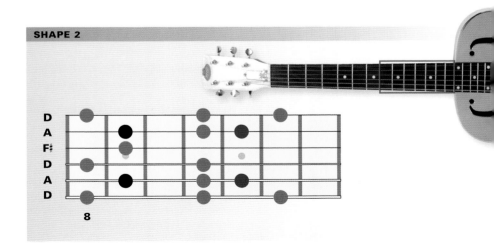

Open D tuning

G major pentatonic

SHAPE 1

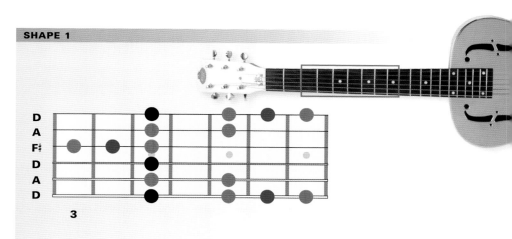

SHAPE 2

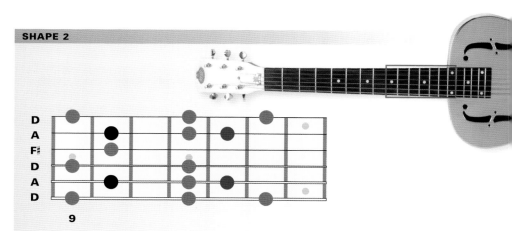

Open D tuning

A♭ major pentatonic

SHAPE 1

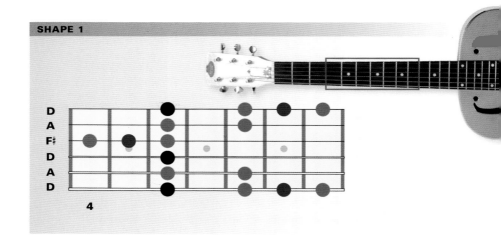

SHAPE 2

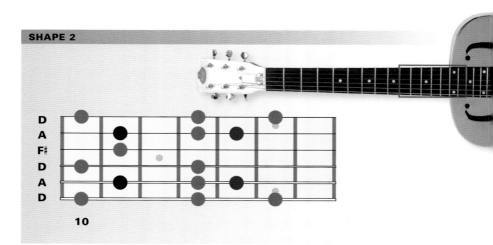

Open D tuning

A major pentatonic

SHAPE 2

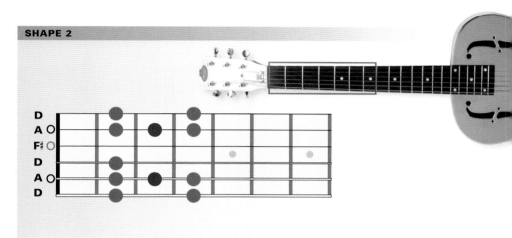

SHAPE 1

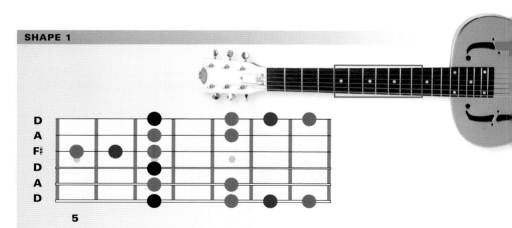

Open D tuning

B♭ major pentatonic

SHAPE 2

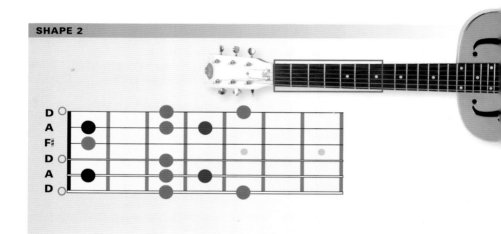

SHAPE 1

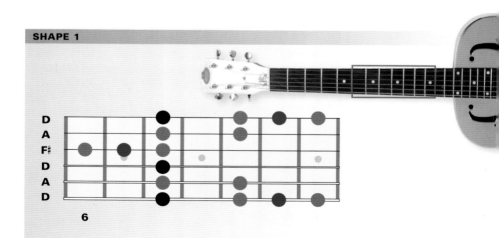

Open D tuning

B major pentatonic

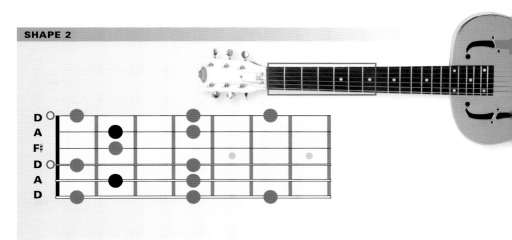

SHAPE 2

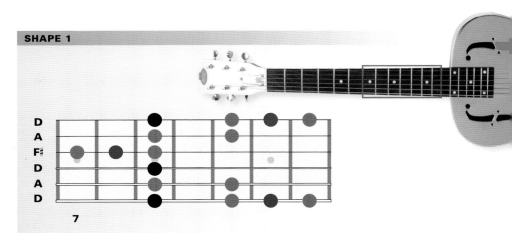

SHAPE 1

Glossary

Arpeggio: Where the notes of a chord are played melodically (i.e. without ringing into each other) as opposed to being played harmonically as in a chord. Arpeggios are invaluable tools for creating melodies and improvisations.

Back beat: A term used to describe the emphasis of the weak beats in the bar (i.e. beats two and four in 4/4 time). The drummer usually plays the snare drum on the back beat to create that all-important "groove."

Barre chord: By fretting across the strings with the first finger, and re-fingering an open chord shape in front of it, a moveable chord shape can be created. The most common barre chords are shape one (based on an open E chord) and shape four (based on an open A chord).

Blue note: Traditionally, this term can be applied to any note that is "worried" by playing it slightly flat or sharp (e.g. by applying a quarter-tone bend to the minor third or minor seventh of the pentatonic scale). However, the term is also applied to the ♯4/♭5 note of the minor blues scale and the ♯2/♭3 note of the major blues scale as in this book.

Damping: Where a string(s) is muted by

quickly releasing the pressure of the fretting hand, or by touching the strings with the picking hand immediately after picking them.

Diatonic: A term applied to any note, interval, or chord that occurs naturally in a major or minor key (i.e. without requiring any scale note to be changed with a sharp, flat, or natural).

Fingerstyle: The technique of plucking the strings with the thumb and fingers, as opposed to using a pick or plectrum. It is a popular technique with country guitarists because melody and accompaniment parts can be played more simultaneously.

Grace note: Distinguishable from a regular note by a smaller print size (and usually with a line through the stem) in conventional notation, or by a smaller print size number in TAB. It is used to indicate the starting note of a non-rhythmical hammer-on, pull-off, or slide, and is played quickly, just before the main note.

Hammer-on: Created by picking only the first of two ascending notes on the same string, the second note is sounded by fretting the note quickly and firmly (i.e. "hammering" the finger onto the fingerboard).

Hybrid picking: A technique first developed by country guitarist Merle Travis. It involves picking a higher string simultaneously with a note played with the plectrum. This is best achieved with your second (*m*) or third (*a*) picking-hand finger.

Inversion: A chord that has a note other than the root note (see Root note on opposite page) as its lowest note. This is frequently the third or fifth but can also be the seventh in a seventh chord.

Legato: A term that literally means to play smoothly or "tied together." Guitarists achieve this by playing consecutive hammer-ons and pull-offs.

Let ring: An instruction usually found at the beginning of a piece of music (in brackets) or under a specific section of music (indicated by a dashed line) to indicate that notes should be allowed to continue ringing where possible (i.e. when on different strings).

Major chord: The major chord is the most consonant (i.e. stable) chord in music. It is a triad constructed from the first, third, and fifth degrees of the major scale. Often described as a "happy" sounding chord.

Minor chord: The minor chord is slightly less consonant (i.e. stable) than a major chord due to the relationship between the root and the minor third. It is constructed from the first, third, and fifth degrees of the harmonic minor scale. Often described as a "sad" sounding chord.

Moveable chord shape: A chord that does not incorporate open strings and so can be played anywhere on the neck. Moveable chords are extremely useful since they allow the guitarist to play in any key. A barre chord is a moveable chord shape but not all moveable chord shapes are barre chords!

Off-beat: When counting in common time (4/4), the off-beats occur naturally between each beat. Counting "+" between the main beats will make it easier to locate the off-beats more accurately. A single bar of 4/4 would be counted as "1 + 2 + 3 + 4 +."

Open chord shapes: A chord played in first position (or with a capo higher up the neck) and incorporating open strings. The five principle open chord shapes are C, A, G, E, and D. Generally speaking, open chords are not moveable.

Palm muting: Where the heel of the picking-hand palm is gently rested on the bass strings just in front of the guitar bridge to create muted bass notes. Used by fingerstyle players to prevent the bass notes from overpowering the melody, and rock guitarists to make the riffs sound more powerful and rhythmic.

Pickstyle: A technique involving the use of a pick (plectrum) to play the guitar's strings.

Pinch: The process of playing two notes at the same time, achieved by picking with the thumb and a finger simultaneously.

Position: This describes the position of the left hand on the fingerboard. In first position, the first finger plays notes on the first fret, the second finger notes on the second fret, etc. So, for example, in fifth position the first finger would play notes on the fifth fret, the second finger notes on the sixth fret, etc.

Pull-off: Created by picking only the first of two descending notes on the same string, the second is sounded by releasing the fretting finger with a sideways "flicking" motion.

Rubato: This literally translates from the Italian phrase *tempo rubato* as

"stolen time." In other words, the musician can freely interpret the written rhythms for dramatic effect. This usually occurs in an intro or ending sequence and without accompaniment.

Riff: An ostinato (repeated) pattern, usually one or two bars in length and often played on the lower strings of the guitar. The introduction to "Smoke on the Water" is probably the most famous example of a guitar riff.

Root note: The note that a chord takes its name from (i.e. the note A in an A major chord). This is usually, but not always, the lowest note of the chord.

Scale: A series of stepwise (ascending or descending) notes that follow a specific intervallic template of tones and semitones. Scales commonly consist of seven notes (i.e. the major scale), but can be fewer (i.e. the five-note pentatonic), or more (i.e. the eight-note diminished scale).

Seventh chord: A basic major, minor, or diminished triad with the seventh interval added (from the root) to create a four-note chord. From the three basic triad forms, four seventh chords can be created: major seventh, dominant seventh, minor seventh, and diminished seventh.

Slide: This is achieved by picking only the first note and then sliding the fretting finger up or down the neck without re-picking. The fretting finger must maintain pressure on the fingerboard when sliding or the second note will not sound.

Slur: A slur is written above or below notes on the stave (as a curved line) to indicate legato phrasing. Guitar players achieve legato phrasing with the use of hammer-ons and pull-offs.

Staccato: An instruction indicated by a dot under or above the note indicating that it should be played shorter than its written value.

Stave: The stave or staff is a system of five lines used to denote pitch in conventional music notation. Specific symbols denote the length of each note or rest (silence).

String bending: Where the pitch of a fretted note is raised by bending the string sharp with the fretting fingers. To add strength, the first and second fingers are usually added behind the third finger. String bends can be any interval from a semitone (one fret) up to a major third (four frets).

Syncopation: The emphasis of "weak" beats to create an interesting rhythm. Weak beats occur on the second and fourth beats (in 4/4 time), or on an off-beat (i.e. occurring on the "and" between the main beats.

TAB: Originally used to notate lute music during the Renaissance, this simplified form of notation indicates where a note should be played on the fingerboard. It does not indicate note duration or rests (silence).

Tone/semitone: The units used to measure the distance between notes. A tone is equivalent to a whole step (two frets) and a semitone a half step (one fret).

Triad: The three notes that make up a major, minor, diminished, or augmented chord. A triad is the result of two thirds stacked on top of each other.

Index

Credits

Quarto would like to thank the following agencies for supplying images for inclusion in this book:

Corbis, p.16
Getty Images, pp.15, 17t, 17b, 46
Rex Features, p.14

All step-by-step and other images are the copyright of Quarto Publishing plc. While every effort has been made to credit contributors, Quarto would like to apologize should there have been any omissions or errors—and would be pleased to make the appropriate correction for future editions of the book.